The Original
Christmas Gift

To Susan — How can I thank you
for your help to me and the parish
over the years? I am grateful to God
for your ministry among us at Ascension.
Dawn joins me in sending our love
at Christmas.

Al and Dawn Lawrence

The Original Christmas Gift

by

Albert S. Lawrence

ISBN- 1-58930-036-0
Library Congress Catalog Card Number- 2001118704

Dedication

To my wife Dawn: Second only to the original Christmas gift, you have always been and will always be my #1 blessing.

To my other four special gifts from God: our children David, Ronald, Kevin and Christin. As God loaned Jesus to Joseph and Mary, so He loaned the four of you to us to raise for Him.

Acknowledgements

My deepest appreciation and thanks to God for those who have assisted me in the preparation of this book and have shepherded it through from start to finish.

Herb Peterson, an avid reader with a keen sense of what makes for good reading, helped me proof read the first draft and shape it in its early stages.

I am grateful also to Flo Harvey, a friend with skill in reading theses. She critiqued the final manuscript and made some significant corrections.

The Rev. Raymond Shaheen, a Lutheran pastor I have known since my college days, offered some key ideas for improvement of the text and format. Because of his example and encouragement years ago, I heard God's calling to serve in the ordained ministry. What a blessing it has been for me to have the privilege of leading people in their walk with Christ during these four past decades!

Rich Lundgren, a journalist by background, read and reread the manuscript in its various stages, each time offering ideas for revision and improvement. To him I owe a special

Acknowledgements

debt of gratitude for his professional expertise and editorial suggestions. His help was invaluable in making the manuscript presentable for publication.

Special thanks goes to my wife, Dawn. She helped continually with organization, proofing, formatting, and computer production. Without her this project would still be on a list of things I would like to do someday.

Contents

Introduction

Where I live in Houston, a festival is presented each year in nearby Galveston called "Dickens on the Strand." Folks dress in nineteenth-century Victorian costume and pretend that the clock has been turned back to Dickens' England. Singers and hand bell ringers come from churches to carol. Vendors sell foods and drinks in keeping with old English traditions. It is a brief excursion into a fantasy world that thousands look forward to each year.

When I attend the festival I can always count on seeing a certain man who dresses up each year as Scrooge. I go up to him and wish him "Merry Christmas!" As you might expect, he remains in character and replies, "Bah, humbug! What is there to be merry about? People spending money they don't have on things they don't need. Humbug, I say!"

I agree. Scrooge is right. Christmas must not be an excuse to go on a spending or partying binge. The meaning is not in the parties nor is it in that cathedral of American consumerism known as the mall. On moving to Houston some twenty years ago, I read that a large new store had opened for the fall season and would be open through Christmas and briefly thereafter. It was called "The Original Christmas

Store." The word *original* intrigued me. I soon learned that to the storeowner it meant simply unique and to my mind, sometimes it meant odd. As I went in I saw the usual collection of nutcrackers, artificial trees, decorations, collections of fruits and foods. But who wants a six-foot elephant made of leather? What did this have to do with the real Christmas? I asked if there were any nativity sets. I was taken to a section in the back where several were available, but expensive. I concluded that this store was "original" in the sense that it did not carry the usual kind of gifts. It was appealing to those who could afford anything and wanted to be truly different.

That store has long since closed. Yet many Americans go on celebrating Christmas and miss its original meaning. How can we rediscover it? How can we keep the yearly tradition of celebrating Christmas from becoming the only reason for the season? We can do it by recapturing and appreciating what God did in coming into the world in person. We can do it by realizing that Christmas is not a fable or sentimental legend but actual historical fact. It is so historical that the entire world lives by a calendar which references what God did on that first Christmas.

C. S. Lewis calls Christmas the "grand miracle." He writes, "They say that God became man. Every other miracle prepares for this or exhibits this, or results from this." [1] Lewis compares it to a book he cannot understand because a very important chapter is missing, a chapter on which the plot of the whole novel is based. Then he finds that missing chapter and he is able to understand everything that went before and came after.

For me the story of Christmas is something like the priceless exhibit displayed in the British Museum in London. It is the Rosetta Stone, discovered in 1799 by a French officer in Napoleon's engineering corps. The stone lay buried in the mud near the Rosetta mouth of the Nile River.

The value of the stone is its carving of a decree by Egyptian priests to commemorate the crowning of Ptolemy V, king of Egypt in the second century BC. One inscription is in ordinary Egyptian characters, another in Greek, and the third in the previously undeciphered Egyptian hieroglyphics. A French scholar first translated the Greek portion. Using that text as a guide he was able to study the position and repetition of proper names and pick out the same names in the hieroglyphic text. He also knew the Egyptian language of his day and this helped him use known words to uncover the meaning of the unknown. By 1822 he finished his work and had the key to the long-lost language of ancient Egypt.

When we begin to understand the story of Christmas, it is as if we have discovered our "Rosetta Stone" to appreciate what God has done on our behalf. The Scripture says that Jesus' birth was, in fact, a gift from God out of undeserved love. "God so loved the world that He gave His only begotten Son, that whoever believes in Him should not perish but have everlasting life" (John 3:16). God did not send us a present. He took the initiative and came in person, wanting us to have the reassurance of knowing who He is and what He is like and how He wants us to live. More than that, what God did in Christ was to provide a means whereby He could justly forgive us our sins.

Yes, **Jesus is the real and the original Christmas gift.** Rightly done, our exchanging gifts with loved ones is a reminder that God gave the greatest gift of all to the "whosoevers" who will accept it and open it. Unlike the gifts we give, this one does not have to be purchased. Yet it is, without any exaggeration, of infinite value and worth. We appreciate it only when we realize how much we need it. All of us have received too many Christmas gifts we neither wanted nor needed. Sometimes we may have caught ourselves opening a present and politely saying, "Just what I needed. Thank you so much." But I can think of more than one Christmas morning when I have said that but was thinking to myself, "What is it?"

Not so with Jesus. If you are breathing, you need the Savior. My hope is that this book will show you the need to hear the message of Christmas and the saving work of Jesus. *Salvation* is a rich word in the Bible. It is used in the broad sense of deliverance from a dangerous situation. In this sense God used Moses to deliver the Jews from bondage in Egypt. In the same way Jesus was born to be the rescuer of all mankind from the penalty and the power of sin and death. This is why the angel spoke to Joseph and said that Mary "will give birth to a son, and you are to give him the name Jesus, because he will save his people from their sins" (Matthew 1:21).

What the Savior came to do is to make us spiritually whole and healthy people. He came to be the doctor of the soul. The gospel message is like a medicine, which heals us and results in our restoration to fellowship with God, the original state in which God created us to live. But as we all know from experience, medicine needs to be applied to do any good. We may have the good sense to realize when we are ill and in need of medical treatment. The doctor may give us sound professional advice and prescribe just the right medicine. We may go and purchase the medicine. But then we must receive it into our body and let it begin its healing work. As long as it is in the container it is a possible remedy, not an actual one. It needs to be taken according to the instructions on the label so as to become absorbed into our body. Then the healing can begin.

The medicine Jesus came to bring was not in a bottle but was his own flesh and blood. His death on the cross was to be the means whereby God could rescue us from the power and

penalty of self-centeredness at the core of our being. This is
the healing everyone needs and which only the Savior can
provide. We receive this healing as we admit our need, and
trust that by going to him in faith he will fulfill his promise
and do his saving work in us. I pray that as you go on with me
in a study of why God sent Jesus on His mission to mankind
you will appreciate more and more of His awesome generos-
ity. I pray that you will be able to say with the apostle Paul:
"Thanks be to God for his indescribable gift" (2 Corinthians
9:15).

Chapter One

The Real Christmas

Christmas is Fact, not Legend

"And it came to pass in those days that a decree went out from Caesar Augustus" (Luke 2:1). We all know the familiar words. Luke is being a careful historian and placing the miracle story of Jesus birth in a historical setting — the time of a Roman Emperor named Augustus. We begin to understand Christmas when we realize that we are dealing with a particular time when God stepped into human history. The Almighty God, for whom time means nothing, became one of His time-bound creatures and was born in Bethlehem.

Every time we date a letter or sign a check we are remembering Christmas. It is now the year 2001. That many years ago in history an event occurred which completely revised the way we mark time. All human history prior to Christmas is "Before Christ" (BC) and history since Christ's birth is "Anno Domini" (AD), meaning "in the year of the Lord's reign." This is powerful testimony that Christmas is not a legend or a fable, which might have begun with the words "Once upon a time…." Rather it is the record of what actually happened in human history. Yet it is more than just human history. It is the unique account of how Almighty God played a significant role in the shaping that history.

Consider how Luke, for example, deals with the task of writing his biography of Jesus: In his preface he states the purpose and method of his compiling his book. Being trained as a physician, he brought to this project the highly developed sense of observation from his practice of medicine. He states in his opening lines that the events he records make up a sacred story about "things that have been fulfilled among us." He comes to his task reverently and delicately as if he knows he is describing sacred history foretold by God.

He also states that he is being careful not to alter what was "handed down to us by those who from the first were eyewitnesses and servants of the word." Just imagine what that involved. He says he has "carefully investigated everything from the beginning" and compiled "an orderly account." He must have traveled to all the cities where Jesus lived and taught and conducted hundreds of interviews with those who knew Jesus personally. We must not forget that this happened in a climate which was hostile to Christianity, where it was illegal to profess faith in Jesus Christ. Many were imprisoned for their testimony, and many died. Yet these eyewitnesses were prepared to suffer and die rather than change their testimony.

Luke is crystal clear about his purpose in writing (Luke 1:3,4). It is not to become a writer of books for a hobby or second career. It is for the sole purpose, he says, of helping his readers in "knowing the certainty" of things that they had been taught. He does not simply want his readers to know the story of Jesus as literature but rather as a message from God Himself.

Luke regards the Christmas story as a news bulletin from heaven. "Unto you is born this day in the city of David a Savior who is Christ the Lord" (Luke 2:11). It is a birth announcement and should be understood as being just that. Suppose you received one in the mail and opened it to read "Jennifer Anne Jones, born on August 20, 2001 to John and Mary Jones. Weight: 6 lb. 5 ounces." You would not say to your spouse, "I don't believe this. They just want us to *think* they have a new baby. It might not be true." No, you would believe the news as documented fact. You could verify it by contacting the couple and going to see for yourself.

When the angel Gabriel announced the birth of the Savior to the shepherds, they intended their message to be received in the same literal and factual way. "For unto you is born this day in the city of David [Bethlehem] a Savior who is Christ the Lord. And this shall be a sign for you; you will find a baby, wrapped in cloths, lying in a manger" (Luke 2:12). Even the angel's announcement contained a direction that they were to go and see for themselves if the news was true.

Another reason for believing that we are dealing here with actual fact is that the narratives given by Luke and Matthew are independent of each other. There is no evidence of collusion or borrowing. Each tells the story from a different angle and seems to be using different sources of information. Each supplements the other. Matthew tells the story from Joseph's point of view, and notes how upset Joseph was on hearing that his fiancée is pregnant until finally he is relieved to hear it explained by the angel. Luke explains how Mary was prepared for the miracle inside her womb and how she humbly submitted to it.

No one knows how Luke and Matthew learned the details about Jesus' birth. I would like to think that before either of them composed their gospel narrative, they got as much first-hand information as they could. Perhaps an elder Mary sat down and related to Luke and Matthew as much as she could remember about the circumstances of the miraculous birth in Bethlehem. Luke tells us that, from that first Christmas on, "Mary treasured up all these things and pondered them in her heart" (Luke 2:19).

Another factor to consider is the rumor that Jesus had an illegitimate birth. Once, when Jesus had boldly declared that certain unbelieving Jews were not acting like true sons of Abraham but like sons of the devil, they retorted by saying, "We are not illegitimate children" (John 8:41). This implied that they thought he was! On another occasion in his hometown of Nazareth when people responded to his teaching with contempt, they asked, "Isn't this Mary's son?" (Matthew 13:55). In a patriarchal society, that kind of insinuation would not have been missed. It was as if no one knew who the father was.

Then, on another occasion when Jesus healed a man born blind, the unbelievers shouted, "We know that God spoke to Moses, but as for this fellow, we do not even know where he comes from" (John 9:29). Rumors about the parentage of Jesus serve only to illustrate the fact that we are talking here about a real birth of a real person whose parentage was open to question. This is more evidence that Christmas is not a myth or legend but the account of a never-before and never-since kind of birth. We call it the virgin birth or, more accurately, the virgin conception.

Whenever I hear the Christmas story read, it always occurs to me that if someone were going to invent a tale or legend it would not come out that way. The circumstances are all wrong. Here we have the story of Almighty God becoming a human being. There is nothing royal about being born in a stable surrounded by animals. How odd that only a

few shepherds should have heard the heavenly announcement. No one would have dreamed of a royal birth happening that way, let alone the birth of a baby who was no less
than God come down from heaven!

We can believe the narrative is historical because there
was no reason to make up such a story. Luke actually says he
is being a careful historian. We find nothing vague about the
story but rather a simple account of what happened. This is
not so with the story of Buddha's birth or the Greek and
Roman legends. Matthew and Luke write soberly, simply and
in straightforward prose. The tone is very Jewish and similar
to the historical accounts in the Old Testament.

We find that the two storytellers did not consult with
each other in their writing, but wrote independently and from
different angles, from different sources of data. Matthew
emphasizes the story of Joseph's dilemma; Luke concentrates
on Mary and on God's selection of her to be the mother of
the Savior of the world. Thus we can safely conclude that
the story of Christmas, set in the days of Caesar Augustus
and Herod the King, is just as historical as events described
in our daily newspaper.

Who Came Down at Christmas?

Quite simply, God did! The words of the carol *Once in
Royal David's City* comes to mind.

> He came down to earth from heaven,
> Who is God and Lord of all,
> And his shelter was a stable,
> And his cradle was a stall
> With the poor and mean and lowly,
> Lived on earth our Savior holy.
> — Mrs. Cecil Alexander

Christmas is the story of God's humbling Himself and leaving heaven to "pitch His tent" here among us. That phrase was the Greek wording John used (John 1:14). It is a mind-boggling miracle. The Creator becomes a creature. Divinity takes on humanity in this unique child who has both natures in one person. This theme is the subject of a famous hymn sung by Christians in the earliest days of the Church. St. Paul gives it to us in the second chapter of his letter to Philippians:

"Christ Jesus, who being in very nature God, did not consider equality with God something to be grasped, but made himself nothing, taking the very nature of a servant, being made in human likeness. And being found in appearance as a man, he humbled himself and became obedient to death, even death on a cross! Therefore God exalted him to the highest place and gave him the name that is above every name, that at the name of Jesus every knee should bow, in heaven and on earth and under the earth, and every tongue confess that Jesus Christ is Lord to the glory of God the Father" (Philippians 2:5-11).

As J. I Packer put it, "The baby born at Bethlehem was God made man."[2] He was not less than God. God could not stop being God. Jesus retained the divine attributes he always enjoyed as God the Son. What he did lay aside were the divine prerogatives and privileges. Honor and glory he left behind in heaven. Jesus donated status and dignity as a price he was willing to pay to go on his mission and to face the hour of sacrifice which that mission entailed.

The passage in Philippians states that Jesus did not count "equality with God a thing to be grasped," that is, held on to for dear life. What it means is that enjoying the honor and glory of being equal with God, as he would later claim in his adult life, was worth laying aside to accomplish the great master plan of salvation for all mankind. For Paul, the thought of what Christ was required to do in order to accomplish this was too wonderful for words. "You know the grace of our Lord Jesus Christ, that though he was rich, yet for your sake he became poor, so that by his poverty you might become rich" (2 Corinthians 8:9).

Christ laid aside his heavenly glory to be born in the humblest of surroundings and without any possessions at all. Yet that condescension to our level, requiring so much sacrifice of heavenly glory, made possible the opportunity for believers to come into an incredible spiritual inheritance. No wonder Paul concluded by saying that the gift of the Savior was beyond human description. Words failed him to convey its reality. He simply said, "Thanks be to God for his indescribable gift" (2 Corinthians 9:15).

To many people the concept of a union between God and a human being sounds like a contradiction in terms. It is like trying to create a square circle. Now while circles and squares are two different shapes, God and man are not shapes at all. God and man are in different categories, and for that reason it is no contradiction to say that Jesus is *both* God and man. He was no hybrid, half God and half man. He was true God and true man, two natures in one person.

The Muslims believe it to be blasphemous to think that God would have a son. On various trips to Jerusalem, which my wife Dawn and I have hosted for groups to see the Holy Land, we have climbed up to the Temple Mount and looked close up at the mosque with the golden dome, a holy shrine for Muslims. Our guide has pointed out that if you look carefully and can read Arabic you will notice this inscription: "There is only one God and he has no sons." The idea that

God could have a son is based on the false notion that this would require a sexual union with a human being. Christians make no such claim. Rather, God in His infinite power bestowed life without having to use any human sexual intercourse.

C.S. Lewis put it this way: "The Second Person in God, the Son, became human Himself: was born into the world as an actual man—a man of a particular height, with hair of a particular colour, speaking a particular language, weighing so many stone. The Eternal Being, who knows everything and who created the whole universe, became not only a man but (before that) a baby, and before that a fetus inside a woman's body. If you want to get the hang of it, think how you would like to become a slug or a crab."[3]

Each Christmas I have looked forward to hearing the newsman Paul Harvey tell "The Story of the Birds." For me it is a memorable word picture illustration of what God was doing in becoming one of us.

"The man's name isn't important ... he could be any number of people living today ... someone who is not some mean, old Scrooge but a kind and decent man who just could not make sense of the story of how God became a man. So when Christmas Eve rolled around this man said to his wife, 'I am sorry to disappoint you, but I am not going to church tonight. I'd feel like a hypocrite because I don't really believe that God became a man. But you go and I'll just stay up and wait for you.' So he stayed home and the wife and children went to church.

"Shortly after the family drove away snow began to fall. He watched the flurries getting heavier and heavier and then he went back to his fireside chair and his newspaper. Minutes later he was startled by a thumping sound, first one and then another, against the living room window. He thought someone was throwing snowballs but when he went to the front door to investigate he found a flock of birds huddled in the snow. In their desperate search for shelter they had tried to fly through his large landscape window.

"Well, he couldn't just let the poor creatures lie there and freeze. He remembered the barn where his children had stabled their pony. That would provide warm shelter if he could just direct the birds to it. Quickly he put on his coat and boots and tramped through the deepening snow to the barn, flung open the doors and turned on a light. But the birds did not go in.

"He figured that food would entice them in. He went back to the house, fetched some breadcrumbs and made a trail of crumbs to the doorway of the barn. But the birds just continued to flop around in the snow. He tried to shoo them into the barn by walking behind them and waving his arms but they scattered in every other direction but the barn. Then he realized that to them he was a large, alien creature. 'If only I could think of some way to let the birds know that they can trust me, that I am only trying to help them,' he thought to himself. Then it dawned on him. 'If only I could become a bird, and mingle with them and speak their language. Then I could tell them not to be afraid, and I could show them the way to the safe, warm barn. But I would have to become one of them so they could see and hear and understand.'

"Just at that moment the church bells began to ring out the song, 'O Come All Ye Faithful.' Finally he realized the truth of the miracle of Christmas. A man's becoming a bird would be nothing compared to God's becoming a man. He couldn't wait to tell his wife and family what had happened while they were at church, and how God had given him an illustration of what Christmas is all about."

For a human being to descend to such a low level of life would be quite a comedown but it is nowhere near the kind of comedown God made in becoming man. For Christmas does not mark the change of one creature into a lower form of creature as would be the case if I were to become a bird or an ant or a slug. No. It is not a higher form of life becoming a lower form. It is the Creator becoming one of His own creatures! Here is how the apostle John put it:

"In the beginning was the Word, and the Word was with God, and the Word was God. He was with God in the beginning. Through him all things were made; without him nothing was made that has been made" (John 1:1.2).

St. Paul wrote: "He is the image of the invisible God, the firstborn over all creation. For by him all things were created, things in heaven and on earth, visible and invisible, whether thrones or powers or rulers or authorities; all things were created by him and for him. He is before all things, and in him all things hold together" (Colossians 1:15-17).

What this means is that we understand Jesus and his mission not in terms of what he said or what he did but primarily in terms of who he was. If we are wrong about Jesus' identity, we no longer have any justification for giving him the kind of honor and worship he has received over the centuries. What relevance could a first-century teacher have for you and me twenty centuries later? The answer is that he has no relevance at all unless he was someone very different indeed. He was more than just the founder of a religion. He was God in human flesh.

The Birthday That Really Wasn't

The Nativity scene with Mary holding Jesus in her arms as Joseph stands nearby is in some respects an ordinary scene. Most of us have had the chance to see and hold a newborn and marvel at the gift of a new life. But Mary's child was different. He who existed from all eternity did not and could not have a "birthday." As God the Son Jesus had no beginning, but he did have an arrival on planet earth. The eternal and ageless deity was now a few hours old. The One who needs nothing was now dependent on his mother's milk. The hands which formed the seas and mountains were now the fists of a tiny baby.

Imagine how Mary, knowing what she did about this unique child, must have felt. I wonder if she ever felt that the God she was praying to was sleeping right in her own home. I wonder if she ever felt awkward telling him Bible stories, knowing he was the author of all of them. I wonder if she might have thought, "That's God sharing a humble meal with us." I wonder if Joseph ever felt strange when Jesus called him "Father."

The songwriter Mark Lowry composed a beautiful melody that makes us ponder these thoughts. It is entitled *Mary, Did You Know?*

"Mary did you know that your baby boy has walked where angels trod? Mary, did you know that when you kiss your little baby you have kissed the face of God? Mary, did you know that your baby boy is Lord of all creation? Did you know that this child you delivered will soon deliver you?" [4]

We cannot know, of course, how Mary felt as she held the baby Jesus in her arms. But she must have replayed in her mind over and over those words of the angel about the way it would happen — by a miracle. If anyone knew that Jesus was virgin born certainly Mary knew it! That is something she would never doubt. She is *the* virgin who would, as Isaiah prophesied long before, give birth to a child who is best described as Emmanuel, "God with us" (Isaiah 7:14).

It is impossible to exaggerate what was involved in Christ's voluntary restraint and laying aside of heavenly glory. For that is just what it took. Christmas marks the act of God deliberately limiting and handicapping Himself to get down on our level as a human being. F.W. Pitt wrote:

"The maker of the universe as man for man was made a curse. The claims of laws which He had made unto the uttermost He paid. The holy fingers made the bough where grew the thorns that crown His brow. The nails that pierced His hands were mined in secret places He designed. He made the forest whence there sprung the tree on which His body hung. He died upon a cross of wood but made the hill on which it stood. The sky which darkened over His head by Him above the earth was spread. The sun which hid from Him its face by His decree was poised in space. The spear which spilled His precious blood was tempered in the fires of God. The grave in which His form was laid was hewed in rocks His hands had made. The throne on which He now appears was His from everlasting years. But a new glory crowns His brow and every knee to Him shall bow." [5]

Now someone may be wondering, "If God really became one of us, how could all of God fit into this human being born to Mary? And if God really did this who was left to run the universe those thirty-three years Jesus was here?"

Throughout the New Testament we are told that Jesus is identified with God without being identical to God. It clearly shows us Jesus acting for and acting as God. He can rightly be called God for he himself claims it. "I and the Father are one" (John 10:30). "If you have seen me you have seen the Father" (John 14:9). He receives worship. He forgives sins, as only God had the right to do. He miraculously heals the sick. He stills the storm. He raises the dead.

But we also find that Jesus prays to God without any suggestion that he is talking to himself. The assumption is that God is in heaven and in full control of the universe while Jesus is on earth. Several illustrations have helped me understand this more clearly, each of which is based on the idea that in Christ we have a sample of deity without having all the deity there is.

I am reminded of a familiar scene at the beach when my children were small. Often they would bring their buckets and shovels and create sand castles. To do that they dug in the wet sand and constructed a castle. Then they would go down to the water's edge and bring back pails full of water for the circular moat. Now ask yourself, is it true that my children have the Gulf of Mexico (or the Atlantic Ocean) in their buckets? Yes and no! The buckets contain some of the seawater and every drop of that seawater is an accurate sample of the vast amount of water in the ocean. The ocean is still as big and deep and wide as before. And yet everything that is in that ocean is also in those buckets.

Dr. Alister McGrath, a contemporary British theologian, develops this concept of Jesus being the "sample" of all that God is.[6] To illustrate he relates the experience of the first astronauts who landed on the moon in 1969. "One small step for man, one giant leap for mankind," the astronaut radioed back as his foot touched the surface of the moon where no human being had ever been before. After the visit was over the Apollo team brought back to planet earth some samples of soil and rock from the place they landed. By means of that sample scientists had an accurate analysis of that soil. You could say that although they had but a small sample of moon rock to take home and analyze, those privileged scientists who examined it in their laboratories were truly examining the true substance of the moon. The moon was still revolving around the earth, but the moon was also, in small samples, in the scientific laboratory, and open to human examination.

In the same way, Jesus is a representative sample of God because he came from God and is identified with God. The incarnation of God, the Christmas story, does not mean that God is confined to and contained only in the human body of Jesus any more than the whole Gulf of Mexico is in the children's buckets, or all of the moon contained in the rock which was brought back to earth. Yet it does mean that, since Jesus is God and comes from God, he and he alone can show us what God is like. God is like the ocean, like the moon, too vast for us to comprehend; so God, in His love for us, makes Himself available to us on terms we can understand and appreciate — by becoming one of us and living among us. To see Jesus is to see God. To obey him is to obey God. To love him is to love God. How good of God to reveal himself in a way we can comprehend.

Note that Christmas is all about God's doing. He takes the initiative. The letter to the Hebrews says that "in times past God spoke through prophets and various ways, but in these days he has spoken to us by his Son, whom he appointed heir of all things, and through whom he made the universe" (Hebrews 1:1). God wanted to say something that written or spoken words could not convey. He came to say that He wants us to know Him and relate to Him the way we relate to another person we know and love. John said it best: "No one has ever seen God: the only Son, who is in the bosom of the Father, has made him known" (John 1:18).

Chapter Two

Where Jesus Came From

If I were to ask, "Where were you before you were born?" you would reply, "Why, for the previous nine months I was growing in my mother's womb." This means, of course, that we are all nine months older than we think. And if I were to carry on and say, "Well, where were you before your concep- tion?" You would answer, "I was nowhere. Life begins at con- ception." And you would be quite right.

Jesus could and did give a different answer. He knew, as he himself declared, that his birth and his conception in the womb of Mary his mother were *not* his beginning. Jesus had no beginning at all. We did; he did not. His conception and birth mark only a stage in his life, his arrival on planet earth where he spent thirty-three years of clock time among us before going back to his heavenly home. His coming among us was, in fact, a temporary visit.

When John wrote his gospel, he thought long and hard how he would begin. He was an elderly man by the time he wrote from the city of Ephesus in Greece sometime between 90 and 100 AD. He wanted to relate the story of Christ but he also wanted to give the story behind the story. He wanted to show that this story was relevant not just to Jews but also to Greeks and all mankind.

Ephesus was a key center in the Roman Empire and to the Greek culture as well. It was in Ephesus that a famous philosopher named Heraclitus lived some five centuries earlier. His view was that everything is constantly changing. He made the famous statement that you cannot step into the same river twice. Life is in flux, like the fire whose flames are constantly in motion. He said that what kept everything together was a divine reason and mind behind all things known as the Logos, or "Word." It was abstract, as Greek thinking was. But it was the key John was looking for. Greeks called the power behind the universe the "Word." Jews called it God. John wrote about God's coming into our world as the time when the Word became flesh. It was as if the abstract principle, the Logos, became concrete. The invisible became visible. The immortal became mortal.

He Left Heaven for Earth

John wanted to emphasize that Jesus lived in heaven before he came to earth. Everything that made God divine was true of him. And then he entered the womb of Mary and became a fetus, attached to her womb, totally dependent on this woman who never had a child, much less this child. We who live in this computerized world marvel at how much information we can get into a tiny microchip. But this is nothing when you think about the Creator of the universe being confined to a few human cells. Imagine it! God the Son spent nine months in total darkness as an unborn baby. But this was not his beginning.

I like the way A.W. Tozer put it: "Time marks the beginning of created existence and because God never began to exist it can have no application to Him. 'Began' is a time word and it can have no meaning to the high and lofty one who inhabits eternity." [7]

In his ministry Jesus offended people by suggesting that he really had no beginning, and therefore only an arrival, not a birthday. "Before Abraham was, I am" He insisted (John 8:58). And as he prayed in the garden of Gethsemane just before his arrest He said, "And now, Father, glorify me in your presence with the glory I had with you before the world began" (John 17:5). Again he said, "I came from the Father and entered the world; now I am leaving the world and going back to the Father" (John 16:28).

So what was Jesus doing before he came into the world? It is hard for us to get out of our time-frame mentality even as we ask the question. But time has no reference point in eternity. So it is we sing in the favorite hymn, "Amazing Grace": "When we've been there ten thousand years, bright shining as the sun, we've no less days to sing God's praise than when we had first begun." Jesus shared with the Father and the Holy Spirit in creating and governing all that is. He was involved in the placement of the planets, the earth, the stars, the moon, the sun, and the galaxies. As John says, "apart from him nothing was made that was made" (John 1:3). Working with wood in the carpentry shop was nothing for Jesus compared to his being part of the creation of the entire world.

Listen to how Paul put it: "For by him (Jesus) all things were created ... things in heaven and on earth, visible and invisible, whether thrones or powers or rulers or authorities; all things were created by him and for him. He is before all things and in him all things hold together" (Col. 1:16). Clearly, Jesus had an important role both in the creation of

the universe and in its ongoing governance. In some mysterious way, everything that exists was hanging together and
operating smoothly because of the supervisory role of Jesus.

On one occasion Jesus noted that some of his disciples
were having a hard time accepting the truth of his symbolic
references to his body as food and to his blood as drink, and
that a disciple will be a person who spiritually feeds on him.
The disciples commented, "This is a hard teaching. Who can
accept it?" Jesus, aware that they were grumbling, said, "Does
this offend you? What if you see the Son of Man ascend to
where he was before?" (John 6:61-62). Heaven was Jesus'
home address.

Jesus himself wanted his disciples to realize that he was
no less than God made man. He had not ceased to be God
but at Christmas he began to be human and had an earthly
address like any one else. J. I. Packer puts it succinctly: "He
was not now God minus some elements of His deity but God
plus all that He had made His own by taking manhood to
himself."[8] Paul's famous passage in Philippians 2 says that
Jesus laid aside the glory he enjoyed with the Father in heaven,
and then emptied himself of the glory and prerogatives that
were his. When he walked around Nazareth, people did not
see a halo over his head. He appeared quite human because
his glory was left behind in heaven. He who had the form of
God in eternity now took on the form of humanity and appeared as a man. As Paul noted, this was God's humbling,
His incredible condescension to our level in order to relate
to us as one of us.

If humility consists of having privileges and laying them
aside to serve others, what more radical example of humility
could we find than this? Existing eternally in the form of
God yet, out of love for us, voluntarily laying aside the pre

rogatives and privileges that were his, Jesus humbled himself to condescend to become one of his own creatures. What a come-down!

He Appeared in a Human Body

The coming of Christ was also a journey from the invisible to the visible. The "Word became flesh..." wrote the apostle John (John 1:1). The Son of God did not have a body before his coming into the world. He was a spirit and only a spirit. You could not see him or touch him because there was no body to see or touch.

Being an invisible spirit, however, did not make him less real. We who live in the twenty-first century understand how invisible things like electricity and radio waves are invisible but very real. Jesus himself used the analogy of the wind when trying to explain the reality of the spirit. We cannot see the wind but we can hear its sound and feel its effects.

The Son of God received his body not in Bethlehem, but at his conception nine months earlier, the moment when human life actually begins. When he was born he looked and sounded like any other baby you might see in a newborn nursery. He wore diapers. He could not feed himself. He was helpless and dependent on Mary and Joseph for everything. He had to learn to speak, to walk, and to experience everything a child does in growing up. He went to school and learned from teachers like every other child in his class. He took no shortcuts around any aspect of becoming a mature adult. Had he done that, he would not be the one who can truly understand and relate to all that you and I experience as a human being

Jesus lived in a body like ours for thirty-three years. It was in this body that he died on the cross, and that he was raised from the dead. It was in this body that he ascended back to his home in heaven. It will be in this same risen and glorified body that one day he will come again to planet Earth, just as he promised. Just think of it! Each of us has the exact same kind of body that Almighty God used to live among us as a human being. That fact alone gives great worth and dignity to our human bodies. If nothing else we should learn from this that all human life is sacred and must never be regarded as disposable or cheap.

He Left Eternity and Entered Time

What about the timing of this journey from heaven to earth? Paul writes that "When the time had fully come God sent forth his son, born of a woman, born under the law that he might redeem those under the law" (Gal. 4:4). He is telling us here that Christmas marks the journey from heaven to earth but also the journey from eternity to time. Heaven is outside of space and eternity is outside of time. This is why Paul writes that God "sent forth his son". Heaven cannot be measured in distance and eternity cannot be measured in time. But the fact remains that His birth happened in history and time, in the world of clocks and calendars. How restricted Jesus must have felt by taking on the limitations of time and schedules.

Christians have always wished that Jesus might have come in their own day. However, we can find several reasons why God decided to send His son when He did. Paul says that it happened "when the time had fully come." What could that mean?

It means that the world was truly ready and ripe for the coming of Christ. He arrived on the world's scene at the opportune moment.

First, on the political scene, the whole Roman Empire was enjoying the "pax Romana," a lasting peace secured by the might of Rome's great military strength. Roads connecting various parts of the empire had been paved and maintained. This was to be a factor in making it possible to spread the news of the gospel far and wide.

Spiritually there was disenchantment among pagan peoples with their gods. Their religions offered no real answers to their deepest longings about the meaning of their lives, and they were open to hearing about a better way. Various secular philosophies were growing in popularity along with the cult of the Roman emperor. This diversity led to greater openness to new ideas. Judaism itself was going through a revival, as we see in the ministry of John the Baptist. The synagogue had also become a common feature of Jewish life and worship. It was the natural place for converted Jews to come and share with others their belief that the long-awaited Jewish Messiah had arrived.

In 280 BC the Old Testament had been translated into Greek, the version known as the Septuagint. More people were receiving an education and many of them knew both Greek and Latin. Common people spoke a dialect of Greek, and it was in this language that the New Testament was composed. In fact Greek had become in that generation what English has become in ours — a universal language. That meant that the apostles could compose the gospels in a language readily understood by people everywhere.

These are a few reasons why the time was both right and ripe for the coming of Christ. There was an actual date but we do not know what it was. We know, for example, from sources outside the Bible that Herod the Great died in the year 4 BC. We also know he was very much alive when Christ was born and when the wise men came to inquire about the birth of a royal child.

This happened because a little-known sixth-century monk and mathematician named Dionysius the Little made history's greatest numerical error in reforming the calendar to pivot around the birth of Christ. Previously the calendar in use was dated from the founding of the city of Rome. We know that Herod died 749 years after Rome was founded and that this date given by Dionysius was 753. The result is that our chronology is actually four to five years off from the actual date of the birth of Christ.

We also know that December 25 is not correct but this is not a problem. Scripture does not tell us the day or month. What happened was that Christians took advantage of being given time off for a pagan holiday celebrating the winter solstice. This meant that Christians could celebrate the birth of Jesus without opposition from the authorities. Thus the early church Christianized a secular holiday.

Is there something wrong with that? For me, everything is right about it. You can actually see that transforming the old and making something new of it is what being a Christian is all about. The word "God" in Greek is a word that in pagan times referred to any god in a vast array of deities, which were supposed to have powers over human lives. Yet when the gospels were written the early apostles used this same word in Greek, *theos,* and associated with it everything about the God of the Bible. We now speak of the study of God as "theology."

Consider also the symbol of the cross. Once it was the symbol of the worst form of torture and death imaginable, a kind of death that the Romans used for the most serious crimes. But God arranged for the Christ to suffer and die on such a cross. Thus a pagan symbol of capital punishment and death was transformed into the symbol of new life and hope, a universal symbol of the Christian faith.

This simply means that Christmas is an undatable date, though it was truly a date in human history. This should not bother us. After all, the Queen of England has a real birthday in April but she celebrates it in June when the weather is better. The meaning of Christmas is not wrapped up in a date but in an action God took on our behalf.

Can you imagine how restricted Jesus must have felt by coming into a world of clocks and calendars, how confining it must have been for him? He had to learn how to tell time like any other boy in Nazareth. He learned about the time to get up, the time to have meals, the time to play and the time to study. He also learned that God expected a time set apart for him, the day of the Sabbath rest. Every Saturday he observed the Sabbath faithfully. Dr. Luke tells us that Jesus worshipped regularly with his parents in the synagogue by custom or habit (Luke 4:16). He also went with them each year to Jerusalem for the Passover festival in the spring. How this reminds us that if we are to be like him we need to give the same priority in our busy schedules to a regular gathering with a body of believers for worship, fellowship, teaching and study.

God's journey from eternity to time has given us the calendar we use every day. We have just begun a new millennium. People all over the world, whether Christian or Jew or Muslim or Hindu or Buddhist or pagan or atheist, all set their watches and clocks and calendars according to that moment in time when God journeyed from eternity into our world of time and space. Each time we write a check or letter we reference that moment when God came to be one of us in Jesus Christ. Let us do it with a brief prayer of thanks that God demonstrated so clearly how much we matter to Him.

Chapter Three

How Jesus Came

What the Virgin Birth Means

Someone once asked Larry King, the popular talk-show host, "If you could select just one person in all of human history to interview, who would it be?" Mr. King answered that it would be Jesus Christ. He followed by saying that he would ask him this question: "Are you indeed virgin born?" The answer to that question, King said, would explain history for him.[9]

Larry King was not being facetious. While a convincing "yes" from Jesus might not truly explain history, it would certainly suggest that we are not bound to find a natural cause for everything that happens. If Jesus is virgin born then it follows that this world of space and time is not the only world there is, and that we need to factor the existence of this other spiritual world into our thinking. It follows that God, the maker of those natural laws which keep this world operating in a predictable and orderly way, could and did deliberately set aside His own laws to enter our world in a miraculous way.

C.S. Lewis, in his definitive book on miracles, pointed out that there is no real conflict between the natural and the supernatural. "A miracle is not an event without a cause or without results. Its cause is the activity of God. Its results follow according to natural law.... If God creates a miraculous spermatozoon in the body of a virgin, it does not proceed to break any laws. The laws at once take over. Nature is ready. Pregnancy follows according to all the normal laws, and nine months later a child is born."[10] In other words, God is the author of both laws, one natural and the other supernatural.

Natural laws tell us what usually happens but not what must happen or how it happens. Natural laws are under God's control because He made them. If He chooses to suspend them for any reason He may do so. This is what happened in the virgin conception of Jesus in the womb of Mary. Joseph was not involved. God dispensed with the need of a male sperm and supernaturally impregnated Mary. In fact, as Dr. Luke tells us the story of Jesus' birth he mentions God no less than fifty-eight times. It is as if he wants us all to know that this is a miracle story from the start.

That is why we must clearly state that the virgin birth is really not about a birth at all, but a conception. Jesus' birth was quite natural and normal, but his conception was not. He was conceived in a supernatural way by a miraculous impregnation by the Holy Spirit. This idea is often mistaken to mean what Roman Catholics call the "doctrine of the immaculate conception." That very different doctrine has to do with Mary's conception one generation earlier. It asserts that God intervened and prevented her from receiving an ordinary human and sinful nature from either of her parents. The logic is that if this were not so, then how could she give birth to a sinless Savior?

However, no scriptural warrant can be found for this belief. We know nothing of Mary's parents or any details about her conception and birth. Catholics are also required to accept the doctrine of Mary's perpetual virginity, a belief that she had no other children after Jesus was born. The mention in the New Testament of Jesus' brothers and sisters is explained away as a reference to children of Joseph by a former wife, or else as his cousins. But there is, as we shall see, a way of accounting for an ordinary sinful human being giving birth to a sinless child. Only God could have thought of it or could have made it happen.

Those who deny the virgin birth of Christ will often say that the account is like Greek myths and legends where various gods with sensual passions come down to earth to make love with women. The offspring is half-human, half-god. Dr. Alan Richardson states: "Pagan mythology is full of legends of a supernatural hero born of intercourse between a god and a human woman. But this is scarcely a virgin birth, and there is no real parallel to the story of the birth of Christ in pagan literature. The Jewish mind would have been revolted by the idea of physical intercourse between a divine being and a woman." [11]

But this is not at all what Matthew and Luke are saying. Jesus is not the product of any kind of sexual intercourse whatsoever, but rather of a unique miracle in Mary's womb. In that way, while not ceasing to be God, Jesus could be truly human in every respect, except that He inherited no sinful nature.

The key verse to understanding this miracle is the announcement to Mary by the angel Gabriel. "The Holy Spirit will come upon you and the power of the Most High will overshadow you. Therefore the child to be born will be called holy, the Son of God" (Luke 1:35). *Overshadow* is such a suggestive word. It is as though a cloud of divine presence would come and surround Mary and by some supernatural process fertilize her egg for this special purpose. This would prevent the transmission to Jesus of the sinful nature which all of us inherit from our parents. Matthew makes the same affirmation in even fewer words. "She was found to be with child of the Holy Spirit" (Matt. 1:18).

We recall that this activity of the Holy Spirit, this overshadowing, was the way the Spirit is described in the activity of creation on the first page of the Bible. There we learn that God created everything out of nothing as the Spirit of God was hovering like a bird providing for and protecting its young. God sent his angel Gabriel to announce that the Spirit of God would also be in the hovering mode as a similar miraculous act of creation took place in Mary's womb.

This is not to say the deity of Jesus Christ is proved by the virgin birth. No such proof is possible. However, we can say that his virgin birth is certainly an appropriate explanation for the entry into our world of such a unique human being. The angel's logic is certainly consistent: "The Holy Spirit will come upon you and the power of the Most High will overshadow you. Therefore the child to be born will be called holy, the Son of God." His natural birth shows us a *real* human being; his supernatural conception explains how he could be sinless and yet be both human and divine. What Jesus is called arose from how he was conceived and born.

We need to say that the virgin birth was no afterthought in God's plan to reconcile us to Himself. As far back as the Garden of Eden we find hints that God would someday send a virgin-born redeemer. After Adam and Eve yielded to temptation God said to Satan: "I will put enmity between you and the woman, and between your seed and her seed" (Gen. 3:15). "Her seed" is used nowhere else in the Bible. Everywhere else "seed" is used of the male, never the female. Only one time do we read of the seed of a woman, and it is in this context. It is a reference forward to Christ's birth without a human father.

In addition to that, God promised that Satan would battle against the woman's seed. This enmity would result in a final confrontation. "He shall bruise your head and you shall bruise his heel" (Gen. 3:15). That is a veiled reference to the cross. The cross is where Satan bruised Christ, but the great victory of resurrection was the powerful blow to the head of Satan, the blow from which he will not recover.

Matthew clearly testifies to the truth of the virgin birth in the first chapter of his gospel, when he is giving the genealogical family tree of Jesus. He traces the line from Abraham going on through David via the family of Joseph. Luke's version is not contradictory. Instead, Luke starts with Jesus and gives us the genealogy of Mary's family back through David and all the way to the beginning with Adam.

There was a good reason for Matthew and Luke to include these genealogies. Because Jesus was born of a virgin and Joseph was not his biological father, he could not be a descendant of David except through his mother. However, the legal right to rule was always established on the father's side, and Jesus was legally the eldest son of Joseph. So we need both of these genealogies. One shows us that through his mother Jesus was a blood descendent of King David, and the other shows that by being the legal son of Joseph, Jesus was properly in the royal line and had the right to rule.

There is an interesting discovery to be made in Matthew's family tree for Jesus. Matthew's genealogical list says A was father of B and B was the father of C, etc. but when he came to the relationship of Joseph to Jesus he changed. In Chapter 1:16 he wrote, "and Jacob was the father of Joseph, the hus-

band of Mary *of whom* was born Jesus, who is called Christ."
When you read this in the original Greek, you notice that
"of whom" is the feminine singular relative pronoun and can
refer only to Mary, *not* to Joseph. This means that Matthew
is saying that Jesus was born of Mary alone and not of Joseph
and Mary. Then, a little later, the angel spoke to Joseph to
warn him of King Herod. The angel said, "Arise, take the
young child and his mother and flee to Egypt." Why did the
angel not say, "Take your child and your wife?" It was because Jesus was God's son, not Joseph's son. A man and a
woman produce only human beings.

Rumors were always floating around about Jesus' parentage. Once, when debating a point with some skeptical scholars, Jesus told them that they were not acting like children of
Abraham but like children of the devil. Angrily they replied,
"We are not illegitimate children," implying by that remark
that they thought he was. And when he went back home to
Nazareth people said, "Isn't this Mary's son?" (Mark 6:3),
thereby insinuating that the father was unknown. Moreover,
when Jesus healed a blind man some hecklers in the crowd
remarked, "We know that God spoke to Moses but as for this
fellow, we do not even know where he comes from" (John
9:29). These innuendoes and insinuations could have come
about only if it was generally known that Mary was pregnant
when she married Joseph.

Someone might be wondering, "Why is there no reference made to the virgin birth except in Luke and Matthew?
The answer is that Mark and John did not include the story
of Jesus' birth and infancy because they chose to start with
the beginning of Jesus' ministry. They did not tell us anything about the childhood of Jesus but that does not mean
that Jesus did not have one. Moreover, the opening lines of
John's gospel tell us indirectly that he did know about the

virgin birth. For example John says that Jesus was "sent by the Father" and "came into the world." Clearly, these are references to Jesus having a supernatural origin.

The parentage issue was one that Jesus dealt with directly in his teaching. Matthew records that when Jesus was talking with the Pharisees, He asked, "What do you think of the Christ, whose son is he?" They said, "The son of David." Jesus then reminded them of how David in the book of Psalms referred to the promised Messiah as his Lord. Jesus asked, "If then David calls him 'Lord,' how can he be his son?" (Matt. 22:43-45). They had no answer.

On another occasion Jesus asked his disciples: "Who do you say that I am?" Only Peter had the right answer: "You are the Christ, the son of the living God" (Matt. 16:16). Jesus said he was right and that God had put that idea into his head. How true. Flesh and blood cannot come to this conclusion. The insight that Jesus is both human and divine, one person with two natures, is an insight given only to those who are open to supernatural leading.

Why the Virgin Birth is Important

You may be asking, "All right, but why is the virgin birth so important?" First of all, it is important because, theologically, it is necessary. It gives us the means by which God became man, which He had to do if He was to bring us salvation. Jesus' natural birth shows us a real human being; his supernatural conception explains how he could be sinless and have a divine nature. An ordinary sinner, however great he might be, however wise, could never offer himself as a sacrifice for sin. Jesus could not be the answer for sin if he were part of the problem.

Here is how Millard Erickson, a distinguished contemporary theologian, puts it:

"For fellowship between man and God to be reintroduced, the gap must be bridged. Someone who is both God and man must bring the two together. If Jesus was not fully God the bridge does not quite meet at the divine end. If he was not completely man, the bridge does not reach to the human side. The full incarnation is not simply a theoretical problem of theology—it is practical necessity upon which man's salvation rests."[1][2]

Our first reason, then, is that the virgin birth shows us how this unique person, Jesus, could be a sinless human being. The sin we find in ourselves was not in him. God, being by nature holy and sinless, could not unite with a sinful being. It is similar to the rejection problem in the transplanting of organs. Our immune system is designed to protect our bodies from infections by rejecting anything foreign. Unfortunately, the immune system regards a donated organ in this same way, as a threat to our health.

The only way doctors can successfully transplant organs is to suppress the immune system by powerful drugs to prevent such rejection. It is much easier when the donor is a relative, as relatives are more likely to have the same basic genetic makeup. The immune system regards the donated organ as no outside threat.

Millard Erickson uses this illustration to say that there is "considerable genetic similarity, as it were, between the deity and humanity of Jesus. He was united with a specific member of the human race who was made in the image of God and free from sin."[1][3] What God did by His "overshadowing" of Mary was the miraculous conception of Jesus in her womb without her ordinary sinful nature being involved in the process. The transplant of the divine seed, then, was made in a compatible way.

Secondly, this "grand miracle" as C.S. Lewis calls it, assures us that Jesus was always who he is. It was not that at some point, perhaps at his baptism, that Jesus became the Christ. No. He was always the Christ, from all eternity, and his conception was not a beginning, as was yours and mine. **His conception and birth were the means of his arriving here from where he had always been — at the right hand of the Father, reigning in power and glory.**

Jesus made such claims about Himself. "I have come from the father into the world; now I am leaving the world and returning to the father" (John 16:28). To his critics he replied, "Before Abraham was I am" (John 8:58). He could just as easily have said, "Before Noah was, or before Adam was, I am."

Paul says that Jesus was "manifested in the flesh," (I Tim. 3:16) and that He "existed from all eternity in the form of God" (Phil. 2:6). Then, when "the time was fully come God sent forth his son, made of a woman" (Galatians 4:4). To be sent forth, the Son has to already exist. Moreover, this previous Christ did not date from creation. For "in the beginning was the Word and the Word was with God and the Word was God" (John 1:1). There never was a time when Jesus was not fully divine. He never became the Christ. He was always God the Son, the second person of the Holy Trinity.

Just think of what Jesus laid aside in order to become man. He did not give up his deity but he did relinquish some of the attributes and prerogatives of deity. Instead of being everywhere at once, now he could be in only one location at a time. He was subject to the limitations of living in a human body just like yours and mine, with its physical need of food and drink and rest. He learned to speak, to read and write. There was no halo over his head, no angel wings on his back. Fishermen felt comfortable in his presence. Even prostitutes felt they had a compassionate listener. Yet all the while He was God in a human body.

Millard Erickson uses a helpful analogy:

"I am reminded of a picnic to which my wife and I were invited when our youngest daughter was in junior high school. Included among the activities was a softball game. There was one unusual feature of the rules that day. The young people were permitted to bat in their normal fashion, but as a means of equalizing the competition, the parents were placed under a handicap. Right-handed batters had to bat left handed, and vice versa (switch-hitters, of course, had a great day). Now one's ability as a right-handed batter was not diminished, but it could not be exercised because of the requirement to bat from the left-handed batter's box. Although one was still able to bat right-handed, one was not allowed to in that particular game, and thus could not bat with the usual effectiveness. In a sense, the limitation was not ultimately physical, for it resulted from a moral limitation. Conscience compelled us to tell the truth about how we normally batted. This is in some ways roughly parallel to what happened in the incarnation. Jesus did not give up the qualities of God, but gave up the privilege of exercising them. Perhaps, at least for a part of his life, he even gave up the consciousness that he had such capabilities and had exercised them with the Father and the Holy Spirit prior to the incarnation."[14]

Thirdly, the virgin birth reminds us that the virgin birth was totally God's idea. It was His action from start to finish. He took the initiative. Notice that the direction of the action behind the event is completely one way! It is a "White House to log cabin story," so to speak. The direction is all from heaven to earth, from Spirit to flesh, from divinity to humanity. There was no 50/50 deal in which God supplied one part and humanity the other part. God was acting as creator, not as a partner with Mary. She merely cooperated.

If there had been some better way for God to accomplish His plan of salvation, do you not think He would have done it? The fact is this method was His choice. There was no easier or better way because of our human situation. This kind of reasoning backwards from effect to cause rather than from cause to effect is an exercise in logic. It means that if you have a very significant effect you can reasonably assume that there is a very significant cause.

Woodcarving ink print by Dawn Lawrence

Chapter Four

The Plan Jesus Followed

He Came by an Eternal Plan

One of the great truths of Scripture is that nothing takes God by surprise. Christmas did not happen as some kind of crisis management on the part of God. His coming into the world was not Plan B. Plan B never existed. The plain fact is that God had Christmas in mind from the beginning. Even in the Garden of Eden God provides a clue that one day in the future the birth of a savior would be announced, a human being descended from Eve who would crush the "head" of evil as one might crush the head of a snake (Gen. 3:15).

What we can say with certainty is that when we speak about God we are speaking about One who knows it all — a God who can see down through the corridors of the future and know everything that is going to happen in advance. He actually said as much. Through Isaiah the prophet, living 750 years before Christ, God said, "I am God and there is none like me. I make known the end from the beginning, from ancient times what is still to come" (Isaiah 46:10).

Here is another astounding claim God makes: **Jesus His Son is the subject of the entire Bible!** Not just the New Testament that was written after His death and resurrection.

Here is how Jesus himself put it. He was speaking to some people who doubted that he had any credentials at all to speak the truth about God. "You diligently study the Scriptures because you think that by them you possess eternal life. These are the Scriptures that testify about me yet you refuse to come to me to have life" (John 5:39).

On the evening of the first Easter, several of Jesus' followers were walking along the road to Emmaus. They were downcast and discouraged from what had happened to their master. As they were talking about the tragic story, the risen Jesus appeared to them as another person walking along the same road. He came up from behind and spoke to them. They did not recognize him because God supernaturally kept them from knowing who it was. Jesus asked what they had been discussing. They were amazed that he did not know the talk of the town, how a man they hoped might be the redeemer of Israel was unjustly put to death on a cross. Moreover, they continued, some women had come with the unbelievable tale that when they went to Jesus' tomb, it was empty but they received word from angels that Jesus was alive. To them the story was incredible.

That is when Jesus replied, "How foolish you are and slow of heart to believe all that the prophets have spoken. Did not the Christ have to suffer these things and then enter into his glory? And beginning with Moses and all the prophets he explained to them in all the Scriptures the things concerning himself" (Luke 24:27).

The walk to Emmaus was about seven miles. The followers and Jesus must have had about three hours for informal Bible study. Imagine Jesus as your Bible teacher! If we were to make sure we examined all the passages in the Bible that are prophecies of the coming of Christ, we would have to deal with at least sixty major prophecies and many other lesser ones.

For our purposes here, let's examine a few of those having to do with his birth, his identity and his ministry.

First, there is the prophecy of where the Christ would be born. The wise men, you remember, came to Herod the king asking about the birthplace. Since he did not know, he asked his Bible scholars. They quoted the prophet Micah: "But you, Bethlehem, Ephrathah, though you are small among the clans of Judah, out of you will come for me one who will be ruler over Israel, whose origins are from of old, from ancient times" (Micah 5:2). Note this: God had accurately predicted the place of Christ's birth and had also said that the ruler to be born there had "origins from of old, from ancient times." Clearly this was a reference to the fact that Christ's birth was his coming into the world from another world where he had been before, the home he rightly called heaven.

Now let's look at some of the major prophecies in the book of one man, the prophet Isaiah of Jerusalem, living in the 750s BC. Many of his prophecies were set to the glorious music of Handel in his well-known oratorio, *Messiah*.

One of the best-known Christmas prophecies is the Emmanuel passage in Isaiah 7:14. Some historical background helps us understand it. In the 8th century BC, civil war had resulted in the split of God's people into two kingdoms, Israel to the north and Judah to the south. Judah was the dominant one. Ahaz was king of Judah. Nations around Jerusalem were gearing up for war because of the rising strength of the Assyrian empire to the east. To protect themselves the king of Israel and the king of Syria entered into an alliance. They invited Ahaz to join the alliance but he refused. As a result

Israel and Syria made plans to attack Jerusalem, remove Ahaz and set up a puppet king they could control. Armies began to assemble and Ahaz was afraid.

That is when the prophet Isaiah went to King Ahaz with a word from the Lord. He said that Ahaz should stand firm and trust God for protection. Sensing Ahaz was reluctant, Isaiah said God wanted to give Ahaz some unmistakable sign, some miracle that would relieve his fears. Ahaz refused, saying he would not tempt the Lord. That was a pious-sounding excuse. The truth is that though he was king of Judah, his faith in God had grown weak. He had tolerated many idolatrous practices and had made many immoral compromises. He was more apt to trust military alliances than to trust God.

Isaiah responded with frustration in his voice. "Is it not enough to try the patience of men? Will you try the patience of my God also? Therefore the Lord himself will give you a sign: (the verb is plural, meaning not just Ahaz but the whole house of Judah): The virgin will be with child and will give birth to a son and will call his name Immanuel." " But before the boy knows enough to reject the wrong and choose the right the land of the two kings you dread will be laid waste" (vs. 14, 16). Who is this child to be born of a young unmarried virgin? It is not sure. From chapter 8 it appears that it is Isaiah's second wife. Apparently his first wife died and he remarried a young woman who was a prophetess. A son was born. The promise came true. Before this boy was old enough to know right from wrong (usually about age twelve) the political picture had changed and there was no longer any threat to Ahaz and the kingdom of Judah. The child did symbolize in a poetic way the truth that God was truly with the people of Judah.

So we see that the Immanuel prophecy had an immediate fulfillment. But God had something bigger in mind. This prophecy was to be **filled fuller** centuries later in the birth of Jesus from a young unmarried virgin without any human father. This would be a miraculous conception with the Holy Spirit as father. Therefore, in the ultimate sense, Jesus' birth is truly "God with us" in a biological, literal way, not merely a symbolic and poetic way. No wonder that Matthew saw the Isaiah prophecy in that light and so recorded it in the Christmas story.

Looking far into the future Isaiah went on to prophecy that "to us a child is born, to us a son is given" (Isaiah 9:6). First of all, notice that this means that the Messiah would be truly human. "For to us a child is born." Jesus was born as you and I were born. He was not half human, and half God. He was 100 percent human and also 100 percent God. For example, in the Apostles' Creed the congregation says: "I believe in Jesus Christ, His (God's) only Son, our Lord. He was conceived by the Holy Spirit and born of the Virgin Mary." God did not exempt Jesus from any experience of being human from the moment he took his first breath. He had all the human feelings, wants, and needs we have. He faced every temptation we face. His body worked exactly like ours. The one thing he did not have was any sin. Yes, he was perfect. He was always right. Imagine being one of his younger brothers or sisters and living in the same home with a perfect brother. Imagine being his mother or stepfather and being given the responsibility of parenting such a child. What an awesome responsibility Joseph and Mary assumed.

Second, he is divine. Note Isaiah's phrase here, "a son is given." That suggests that Jesus already existed in heaven before he was born as a man. He had no beginning in time at all, only an arrival to planet earth where he paid a thirty-three-year visit. He was the true extraterrestrial who could actually say he was from elsewhere, even from heaven where he had been from all eternity. This is the other half of Jesus' identity, his other nature. He was God in a human body.

Third, Isaiah says, "The government will be upon his shoulders." He did not mean an earthly government but a spiritual one. He will be rightly called a king yet he would later testify to Pontius Pilate, the Roman governor, that his kingdom is not of this world. Jesus came to rule in the hearts and souls of those who want to come under that rule. The trouble with many of us is that we want to be our own king and CEO. God never intended that for anyone. Rather, He expects that if we believe in Him as God we will let Him be God. That means that we are to submit voluntarily to His rule and relate to Him as our King, doing His will on earth as gladly and enthusiastically as it is done in heaven. When this happens the government of our lives is no longer on our shoulders but His. As a result God can guide us to make decisions that are both right and good for us and are also pleasing to Him.

In perhaps less detail, Jesus would then have gone on to mention Isaiah's other titles for the Christ. "And he will be called Wonderful Counselor, Mighty God, Everlasting Father, Prince of Peace. Of the increase of his government and peace there will be no end" (Isaiah 9:6).

The Messiah turned out to deserve all those titles. The apostle John wrote of Him, "No one had to tell him what people were like. He already knew" (John 2:25). That is why Jesus was and is the greatest psychologist and the most wonderful counselor the world has ever known. And before Jesus died he promised to ask the Father to give the disciples "another counselor to be with you forever, the Spirit of Truth" (John 14:6). The word *another* means "one of the same kind," not a different kind. That means you and I also have access

to this wonderful counselor of God who gives wisdom, guidance and assurance right now. He is the Holy Spirit, God by
another of His names.

Just what is a counselor? A counselor is someone who
can clarify issues for us and help us make right decisions. He
is also one who teaches, not as an instructor in front of a
class, but one on one with a person who needs guidance. A
counselor is also a person who comes alongside another person for support. The Greek word for the Holy Spirit is a word
that means just that: "one who comes alongside."

The retired Episcopal bishop of Colorado, William Frey,
tells a story that illustrates this point. When Bishop Frey was
a young college student he spent one afternoon a week reading to a boy named John who had lost his eyesight. When
the accident happened, John thought his life was over. He
was mad at the world and mad at God. He shut himself in his
room and came out only for meals.

"One day," John later said, "my father came and gave me
a lecture. He told me to stop feeling sorry for myself. He felt
it was time to move on with my life. He asked me to find a
way to get the storm windows up before cold weather arrived.
It made me angry. So I groped my way to the garage, found
the tools and went to work. I even hoped I would fall off the
ladder and break my neck just to make him sorry. But I managed to get the job done." Then John paused as his sightless
eyes began to get teary. He went on to say, "Later I discovered that at no time during the day had my father ever been
more than five feet away from my side!"

Bishop Frey commented, "I have no idea whatever happened to John, but I will always remember him. He thought
he was telling me a story about his father. In reality he was
telling me a story about the Holy Spirit. Every time that I
have wanted to ask, 'God, where were you when I needed

you the most?' I would remember John. And I can just hear the Holy Spirit saying, 'Never more than five feet from your side!'"

Jesus the Wonderful Counselor is still available to us in the person of the Holy Spirit. He took up where Jesus left off. No appointments are needed. No fees are required. We have full access to this Wonderful Counselor today if we will just be sure of one thing. We need to let Him have full access to us.

Then notice that Isaiah promised that the child would be "mighty God." Jesus claimed to be no less than God in human form. "If you have seen me you have seen the Father," He said to Philip (John 14:9). Christmas is not the celebration of the birthday of the greatest man who ever lived. It is the celebration of the coming of one among us who was no less than Almighty God. Jesus made it clear that whatever a person thought of him was what that person thought of God. To love him was to love God. To know him was to know God. To reject him was to reject God. Jesus not only acted as God; he claimed he was God in so many words and on various occasions. Sometimes the claim was implied; sometimes it was stated outright. This offended some of his critics who interpreted his comments as "making himself equal with God" (John 5:18). To them it was outright blasphemy, yet it was actually the mysterious but literal truth.

Recently I was in a cafeteria line at a local restaurant when I noticed that the man serving me my food had on a nametag that said, "Jesus." In the Hispanic community the name is actually quite common. It was also common in Jesus' own day. The name sounded as Yeshua. Our word Jesus in English comes from the Greek translation of this name which was derived from the Hebrew name Joshua, meaning "God saves." We also read that St. Paul had a friend named Jesus

Justus. The point is that this mighty God of ours came into the world and wanted to be called by a name that was common, one which would be called out several times in any class roll. What this tells me is that Almighty God wants to be approachable. Never do we read that after any of the mighty miraculous acts of Jesus caused people to be afraid of him. He was mighty God all right, but he was careful never to use his divine power just to get people's attention or to threaten them but rather to give them clues as to his real identity.

Jesus went on to remind his two walking companions that Isaiah promised the child was to be the "everlasting Father." To think of God as "Father" was a new idea in Jesus' day. Yet it is the one word picture that is consistent in all of Jesus' teachings about God. It is how we are to think of God in the model prayer he taught us to use. The image of God as our heavenly Father brings to mind the provision and protection God wants to give us, and the caring role He always assumes.

But don't gloss over that word "everlasting." What in this world do you know that is everlasting? Everything is changing. Think of the way computers have changed our lives. Consider the tearing down of the Berlin Wall, the fall of the Soviet Union and the end of the Cold War. Think of space exploration. Think of advances in the medical field.

But would you want a God who changes or needs updating? If God is perfect, then any change would be for the worse, not the better. And when it comes to God, there is no need to change. God is not somehow slowing down or growing weaker. He does not age, as humans do. The passing of time has no effect on Him. This is what we mean when we sing the doxology in our worship: "Glory be to the Father and to the Son and to the Holy Spirit. As it was in the beginning, is now and ever shall be, world without end. Amen." Through the prophet Malachi, God said, "I am the Lord, I do not change" (Malachi 3:18). This is what the author of the letter to the Hebrews meant: "Jesus Christ is the same, yesterday, today and forever" (Hebrews 13:8).

What this means in practical terms is that God is never going to stop loving and caring and being gracious to us. For me this is the basis of my feeling secure in a world of change and uncertainty. It means that I can pick up a book called the Bible, written thousands of years ago, and believe that what was written for people back then is written for people like me in my generation. It is all because God is from everlasting to everlasting, always the same. Jesus came to proclaim this God whose character is perfect and unchanging, and who wants us to think of Him in the caring and providing role of Father.

Jesus went on to comment on Isaiah's promise that the child would be the "prince of peace." Remember how the Christmas angels announced that the birth of Jesus would herald a coming of "peace to men on whom his favor rests" (Luke 2:14). This is a more accurate translation than the King James Version's "peace on earth, good will towards men." There was no "blanket" of peace and goodwill dropped from heaven to earth at the birth of the Savior. Hardly. Yet Jesus could rightly claim to be Prince of Peace through his primary role of being the reconciler of human beings to their God. It was the end goal of his entire ministry, and it took a cross to make it happen. God's favor does indeed rest on any of us when we trust in Jesus as Savior, and believe that it was for our sins that he died on Calvary's cross. That is the true secret of genuine, lasting inner peace.

Isaiah had also said that the Messiah would "bear the government on his shoulders." It would not be an earthly government, but the government of individual lives who choose to come under the kingly rule of Jesus Christ. He came to do this for followers in every generation. The trouble with so many people is that they are president and CEO of themselves. God never asked that of anyone. He wants to govern our lives but He will not force Himself on anyone. Earthly kings and monarchs are not elected. But in the kingdom of God there is an election of Jesus as King in the hearts of every one of his subjects. There is no pressure on any of us to come under his gracious rule. There is only an invitation for us to give him permission to take the government of our lives upon his shoulders and for us to call him King and Lord.

When Jesus got to the famous prophecy of the death of Christ in Isaiah 53, he must have told the two followers on the road that this passage was describing the purpose of his mission on earth. This was the "hour" for which he was born. "He was pierced for our transgressions, he was crushed for our iniquities; the punishment that brought us peace was upon him, and by his wounds we are healed. All we like sheep, have gone astray, each of us has turned to his own way; and the Lord has laid on him the iniquity of us all" (Is. 53:6). Somehow that verse says it all.

He would also have noted Isaiah 61 where the prophet lays out a kind of blueprint for the ministry of Jesus. "The Spirit of the Sovereign Lord is on me, because the Lord has anointed me to preach good news to the poor, to bind up the broken hearted, to proclaim freedom for the captives, and release from darkness for the prisoners..." He surely reminded them of that day in Nazareth when he was about to begin his ministry. He was asked to read from Isaiah that day and He chose these very verses, and then adding his comment: "Today this scripture is fulfilled in your hearing" (Luke 4:21).

As the three walked along and Jesus was interpreting the passages in Scripture that pointed to his birth, his ministry and his death, they reached their destination. They invited Jesus to come in for a meal. No doubt they hoped to hear even more Bible interpretation. Jesus accepted and came in. Then, as they were ready to eat, Jesus took bread, broke it and gave it to them. That was when God opened their eyes to see the real identity of their guest. It was the risen Christ, and they recognized him. But that is when he chose to disappear from their sight. He left them amazed, and ready to believe that he really was alive again in some new and mysterious way. Then they remarked, "Were not our hearts burning within us while he talked with us on the road and opened the Scriptures to us?" (Luke 24:32).

What this means is that Jesus came by an eternal plan in the mind of God. It was this plan that was in operation long before the first Christmas, even from eternity. It was the plan Jesus was following when he left the carpentry shop and inaugurated his ministry where John was baptizing in the river Jordan. It was the plan in place when he called his disciples, when he taught in parables, when he healed the sick, when he performed the miracles. It was the plan behind the confrontation with the religious authorities as he dared to call himself God. Jesus voluntarily surrendered to arrest, knowing that if he wanted, he could call legions of angels to bring it to a halt. It was the plan when he was intimidated and whipped at the hands of a cowardly Roman governor interested more in crowd control than in truth and justice. It was the plan being followed when Jesus died on the cross and when three days later he rose from the dead and convinced his followers that he was alive again. It was the same plan that took him back to his heavenly home at the Ascension, and from which, as he promised, he will one day come back again, this time in great power and glory.

What does this mean for us? It means that we can believe that, although to our human mind and viewpoint things happen with no rhyme and reason, we can believe that God is in control. He always has been; He always will be. He sees the big picture; we see only a corner of the canvas. He is never taken by surprise.

The good news is that much as we might like to know the answer to the oft-asked question *"Why?"* All we need to know is the answer to the question *"Who?"* Jesus came at Christmas to be the answer to that question. The kind of God we see in Jesus is both conscious of world history and in complete charge of it. That being so, we know that God is aware and concerned about what is going on in our lives. We can believe that God is both the author of history and the goal toward which history moves year by year. As the saying goes, "We may not know what the future holds, but we know Who holds the future." And He is trustworthy.

Chapter Five

Why Jesus Came

He Came to Seek and Save the Lost
"For the Son of Man came to seek and save what was lost" (Luke 19:10).

We learn the reasons why Jesus came as we allow the Scriptures to give us direct and unequivocal answers. First of all, we remember how the angel announced to Mary that her child would "save his people from their sins." Remember how the angels told the shepherds that in Bethlehem they would go and find a special baby who is a "Savior, Christ the Lord"? Jesus came to the world's rescue to save mankind from the consequences of sin. That is why we say in the words of the creed, "For us and for our salvation he came down from heaven and was made man..." He is God's answer to a human problem that we were helpless to solve.

Rescuing the lost sheep is what shepherds do, and Jesus likened himself to a good shepherd, searching for lost people. Even as I say "lost" in this context I realize that many people today do not understand the way in which Jesus meant it. It is clear from Jesus' teaching that when a person is not close to God, he or she is, in fact, lost. Sheep do not deliberately decide to stray from the flock. What usually happens is that a sheep will find something interesting to go and look at, something to nibble at, and thereby wander away unconsciously and often into danger.

People act in the same manner. We too "have erred and strayed from thy ways like lost sheep" as the Anglican Book of Common Prayer puts it. Isaiah said it so memorably in his famous 53rd chapter, verse 6: "All we like sheep have gone astray..."

When Jesus said he came to seek and save the lost, he had just had an encounter with a tax collector named Zacchaeus. Jesus was passing through Jericho, where Zacchaeus lived and worked, and Zacchaeus wanted to observe Jesus first hand. Being short of stature, he climbed a sycamore tree to get a good look. Imagine his surprise when just as Jesus came near the tree he called to Zacchaeus by name and invited himself to dine at Zacchaeus' home. Being completely despised and friendless because of his occupation, Zacchaeus was delighted that someone wanted to befriend him. I have often wondered why Jesus singled him out. I believe it must have been that Jesus recognized in him the attitude of many people today. Here was a man who could say, "I've been there, done that. Is there anything more to life I don't know about?"

Luke condenses the story (Luke 19:1-10). They go home, sit and eat a gourmet meal. But what did they discuss? Did Jesus ask, "How is your marriage? Do you have any real friends? Tell me about your family. Is your wealth bringing you happiness?" We will never know. My hunch is that Zacchaeus himself was the agenda.

What we do know is that by the time the meal was over, Jesus had changed this man from the inside out. "Zacchaeus stood up and said to the Lord, 'Look, Lord! Here and now I give half of my possessions to the poor, and if I have cheated anybody out of anything, I will pay back four times the amount'. Jesus said to him, 'Today salvation has come to this house, because this man, too, is a son of Abraham. For the son of Man has come to seek and to save what was lost' " (Luke 19:10).

It is good news to realize that we needn't remain what we are. People can begin again. And notice that in this case it was a kind of double search — Zacchaeus looking for Jesus and Jesus looking for Zacchaeus.

We can all identify with times we are lost — in the woods, or in a strange city. We need someone who is familiar with the place to give us directions. We also know about losing valuables. Perhaps they are stolen or misplaced. When I can't find something you might hear me mutter, "Nothing is ever lost, only misplaced." It is not where it ought to be. Finding it means getting it back where it belongs.

For more than a year my wife Dawn could not find her diamond engagement ring. She had taken it off because several of the prongs holding the diamond were broken and it was loosely mounted. So she found a safe place to put it while we were on an extended vacation. The hiding place was so safe that when we came back she could not remember where she put it. The two of us turned the house upside down trying to locate it. We had given up on it when one day, cleaning a drawer, she discovered the ring. It was hidden under the drawer paper. You can bet there was rejoicing that day when she announced the ring was found!

God is a God who searches after lost people because they matter to Him. In the parable about a lost sheep, Jesus makes it clear that God never writes off the lost sheep as being dispensable. Nor is anyone so lost that he or she is irretrievably lost.

Jesus came to seek out the Zacchaeuses in every nation and generation — the people who have everything and nothing at the same time. The only redeeming quality about Zacchaeus was that he did not pretend everything was fine, as many lost people do today. Worse still is the tragedy of being lost and not knowing it. Sometimes lost people keep each other company and there is no one to confront them with the truth. But lost people cannot fool themselves forever, and they begin to realize that they have been living in denial a long time.

God wants to seek after you and find you. You may have been nibbling your way from pasture to pasture, searching here and there for something that really brings meaning and satisfaction to you. You may feel the lostness of not being special to any significant person, and you are truly lonely. You may have failed to measure up by reason of something said or done. The lostness of broken relationships with other people, and especially with God, is a painful experience.

The good news is that it does not matter to God how lost a person is. What matters is the search and rescue. "What man among you, if he has a hundred sheep and has lost one of them does not leave the ninety-nine in the open pasture and go after the one which is lost until he finds it?" (Luke 15:4) Picture the shepherd striding back to his friends as they welcome him with cheers. "Rejoice with me," he calls out, "for I have found my sheep which was lost" (Luke 15:6). That is how it is with God and us. God came into the world on a search and rescue mission for lost people. He took the first step to look for us. Our part is to seek for Him even as He seeks for us. In that meeting we will find the happiness we have not found anywhere else.

He Came to Testify to the Truth

"For this reason I was born and for this I came into the world, to testify to the truth" (John 18:37).

The context of this statement comes during Jesus' trial before the Roman procurator, Pontius Pilate. Pilate is investigating his claims. "You are a king?" he asked. Jesus replied, "You are right in saying that I am a king. In fact for this reason I was born and for this I came into the world, to testify to the truth. Everyone on the side of truth listens to me" (John 18:37).

Did you catch the assumptions in that statement? If we can be both on the side of truth and able to bear witness to it then there must be something objective about it. It must be discovered and not invented. It must be true whether we know it or not and whether we like it or not.

Christianity stakes its claim on its being true regardless of any human opinion. In fact Jesus was bold enough to say, "I am the truth" (John 14:6). No one had ever said that before. Not Plato or Aristotle or Socrates. They were wise enough to realize that they had learned only a fraction of all the truth there is. But Jesus could honestly say that he is truth. And he could say it because of who he was.

Here is something all of us should ponder: Whenever we are seeking after truth, we are seeking after God, because all truth is God's truth. Jesus actually claimed that, too. When he was about to end his life on earth and return to heaven he promised his disciples that they would not be on their own. He would send them a counselor, the Holy Spirit, God by another name, who would "guide them into all truth." Note the word *all*.

Today you and I live in a culture that looks askance at anyone who says that truth is objective and given. Rather, the popular understanding is that I have my truth and you have your truth, and the goal is for us to get together and agree of what we would call "our" truth. To many people truth is like beauty, in the eye of the beholder. It is like one flavor of ice cream we prefer over some other flavor. We recall the old saying, "There is no disputing about taste."

I grew up just outside our nation's capital in Washington, D.C. Often I would pass by the building of the Bureau of Standards where there is a room which houses the original, authentic weights and measures we use every day. I have never heard anyone say that there is anything wrong with that. I do not hear about someone wanting to change the inch, the foot, the pound or the gallon to some other weight or measure. Now while these standards are not divinely given, we have the good sense not to try and revise them.

Imagine the chaos resulting from a gallon meaning four quarts in some states and five quarts in others. Imagine how impossible it would be for a contractor to build a house if some workers were using a measuring tape where a foot is twelve inches and others were using a tape where a foot is fifteen inches. No, measurements are valid insofar as they are faithful to the original standard everyone agreed on.

In the same way, we tell truth from error, right from wrong, by measuring against a standard that is original and authentic. Webster defines *truth*, in part, as "fidelity to an original standard." God is that standard. If we are concerned about what is fair and unfair, it is because God is also. If we think love is good and hate is bad it is because God does also. If honesty is right and deceit is wrong it is thus simply because God says it is.

During World War II, Adolf Hitler created belt buckles for his soldiers with the words inscribed, "Gott Mitt Uns" (God With Us). That may have been his wish but it was not the truth. Our concern must never be that God be on our side. No, our concern must be that we are on God's side! And how do we know what side that is? We can know only as God shows us in terms we can understand. Jesus came into the world to do just that. "No one has ever seen God; the only Son who is in the bosom of the Father, he has made him known." (John 1:18) Catch that phrase, "made him known." Jesus is saying that we would never have known God accurately and fully unless Christmas happened. God came into our world in the person of Jesus to give us a clear and full understanding of His nature, as much as our finite minds can comprehend. He did not let us figure out His truth as best we could. He is not playing hide and seek. Christmas says He wants us to know the truth about Himself, our world and ourselves.

Jesus said to Pilate, "Everyone who is on the side of truth listens to me" (John 18:37). Note what that implies. A thing is true not because Jesus said it. Jesus said it because it is true. That also means that a thing is right not because it is Christian; it is Christian because it is right. Jesus did not come into the world to bring a brand new edition of morality and truth, but to illustrate the objective truth that was already there. That is why anyone who is honestly seeking to know what is truth is actually looking for the one who embodies all truth, namely Jesus Christ.

When we are ill we know that there is a reality called medical science that can help us. But that reality becomes more real when we encounter it in the person of a doctor or nurse. Likewise, the Bible contains correct statements about the nature of God, our world, and us. But how much more credible are those statements when they are personified in the figure of a human being like ourselves.

What this means is that truth is not an abstraction such as Pontius Pilate thought. It is not information, either. Our information technology society needs to hear that. No, truth is to be found in a person who can say what no one before or since could say: "I am the truth." That is why we cannot learn the truth Jesus came to proclaim and say, "Isn't that interesting?" We have to make a choice. We can give in to the culture and believe that truth is relative and subjective, no more than a personal preference and taste. If we do we shall fit right in. The other choice is to believe that truth is truth regardless of anyone's choices. Jesus alone can show us that unchanging truth of God and the value of making all our decisions on the basis of it.

He Came To Give His Life as a Ransom

"For even the Son of Man did not come to be served, but to serve, and to give his life as a ransom for many" (Mark 10:45).

It would certainly be a mistake to try to find significance in the Christmas event alone, disconnected with the cross of Christ and his voluntary death on our behalf. In other words, Jesus was born to die! He came to reveal the nature of God, to teach and to heal, but his main purpose was to take upon himself our sins and suffer the penalty those sins deserved.

The disciples never did grasp why their Master was voluntarily laying down his life when he could very easily have avoided his suffering and death. He gave up his life willingly, as he himself said (John 10:17-18). He paid the price of death, thus making it possible for God to remain just and still give us His pardon.

But someone may be asking, "If God wanted to forgive people why did He not just go ahead and announce it? After all, the Bible says we are required to forgive one another and we are warned of dire consequences for refusing to forgive. Why can't God practice what He preaches? Why is someone's death required?"

The answer is that there is no parallel between God and us when it comes to forgiving. It is not a question of one sinner forgiving another sinner. It is a matter of sinners having offended a just and holy God. How could God forgive without compromising His holiness? Suppose a criminal court judge felt sorry for an offender convicted of a crime and he wanted to release him as an act of mercy. If he did, what would become of the justice system he was elected to uphold? But suppose that same judge, after imposing the fine on the defendant, reached into his pocket and wrote a check for the full amount on his own bank account. This is a clue to what was happening on the cross.

Another word picture Jesus used to illustrate what he came to do is found in Mark 10:45. He said he came to give his life "as a ransom for many." We also find this image in the writing of Paul where he says that Jesus Christ is "a mediator between God and men, the man Christ Jesus who gave his life a ransom for all men" (I Tim. 2:5,6).

The word *ransom* denotes the idea of setting free that which was formerly captive. Usually we think of ransoms in terms of criminal activities, such as the famous case of Charles Lindbergh, the aviator, whose baby boy was kidnapped. Then the ransom note was sent to the Lindbergh family with a demand for monetary payment for the release of the child.

We ask, "How could the death of Jesus be a ransom?" In Bible times the concept was quite familiar to people, as familiar to them as it is strange to us. Moses had decreed that if a man owned a dangerous bull and it gored somebody to death, the owner's life was in jeopardy unless he came up with the ransom price. In the same way a poor Israelite might be forced through debts to sell himself into slavery. Later he could be "redeemed" or bought back by a relative for a certain price.

The thought here is that human beings are in a moral and spiritual bondage and cannot get free by themselves. Do you remember how Jesus once asked, "What can a man give in exchange for his soul?" (Mark 8:36) The implied answer is "Nothing." All you and I can contribute to our salvation is the very sin from which we need to be saved! God did it all. He met his own demands. Jesus gave his life for many, one dying for a multitude, his single life given for the plural lives of all mankind.

You may be wondering, "If Jesus' death was truly a ransom, to whom was the ransom paid?" In the case of the Lindbergh kidnapping it was very clear where the money should go, namely to the kidnappers, the criminals involved. They set the amount of money required and they were ready to release the child when the payment was made. Unfortunately, the money was paid but the child, whether deliberately or accidentally, was killed.

On the cross of Christ there is no third party. It is certainly not the devil, for if it were, that would clearly show that the devil won. The clear message of the Christian faith from the very beginning is not that the devil won but that Christ won. The proof was the resurrection of Christ from the dead.

No, the best we can say about the ransom of Jesus was that it was the mercy of God meeting the demands of the justice of God. As we have seen God is both the judge and the injured party. In order for there to be forgiveness for me as a sinner, God had to decide He would accept a substitutionary payment for my sins. God does not negotiate away His justice. Therefore the fact that my debt is paid and my

Why Jesus Came

sin is forgiven shows that in the cross there is perfect justice and perfect mercy. As the saying goes, "He came to pay a debt he did not owe because we owed a debt we could not pay."

Just think about the price God paid to free mankind from the bondage of sin. It was the death of His one and only Son. What does that tell us? It tells us that we matter that much to God. Throughout the New Testament the idea of being set free from the bondage of sin and death is everywhere the joyful note. God wants us to realize that His mission in coming to save us was a mission of liberation. We could not set ourselves free. God intervened and released us by the cross into "the glorious liberty of the children of God" (Romans 8:21).

If the sins of mankind were "no big deal," God would not and should not have had to come into the world and suffer and die for them. Obviously there was no easier way. Yes, as Paul put it, "Christ died for sins, and not for ours only but for the sins of the whole world" (I John 2:2). Personalizing it and claiming Christ as his own Savior, Paul wrote: "I am crucified with Christ, nevertheless I live, and the life I now live in the flesh I live by faith in the Son of God who loved me and gave himself for me" (Gal. 2:20). Peter was equally emphatic: "Christ died for sins, once for all, the righteous for the unrighteous, to bring you to God" (1 Peter 3:18).

He Came to Bring a Sword
Jesus said, "Do not think that I have come to bring peace on earth; I have not come to bring peace, but a sword." (Matt. 10:34).

Really? That saying of Jesus sounds out of character. It sounds as though he is advocating conflict. Luke's gospel quotes Jesus as saying that he came to bring division. And

Jesus seems to be saying that he came to set people against each other, even in a family. How could this be? I thought the angels spoke of peace on earth at his birth. And did Jesus not say that the truly happy ones would be the peacemakers? And didn't Paul say that the ministry of the gospel was about reconciling people to each other?

What then is this talk about Jesus bringing a sword and about his creating tension and conflict among people? First of all, we can say that when he spoke about conflict within a family, he spoke from personal experience. Members of his family of brothers and sisters did not automatically support him. On one occasion they said he was beside himself and tried to call him home from a gathering where he was teaching. John the apostle says, "even his brothers did not believe in him" (John 7:5). Later on we read that one of his brothers, James, was converted when the risen Christ appeared to him. James then became a believer and leader of the church in Jerusalem.

Experience confirms this truth: Christ invites everyone to believe in him, but some will choose not to believe. So when Christ came to bring a sword it means that this is the net effect of his coming, not his purpose. We know this to be true. You may have a parent who is a committed believer and the other parent is not. The same is true for a brother or sister or a son or daughter. It proves that deciding to be a Christian is a decision only an individual can make. Wouldn't it be great if this were not so? Would it not strengthen the cause of Christ if people would inherit the faith genetically?

The answer is no. It is said that God has no grandchildren. It is always a first-generation experience. You can never borrow it nor inherit it. That is not how God works and I am glad of it. Let me tell you why. I do not want anyone doing my believing for me and I cannot do anyone else's believing.

Likewise I cannot do anyone else's confessing. How would you like living in a world where someone would say, "I'll take that microbiology exam for you" or "I'll go through that chemotherapy for you"? You'd be OK with that. But it would be a world where someone would also say, "I'll take that Caribbean cruise for you" or "I'll take that promotion for you." No, you would not be OK with that. The point is that choosing Jesus Christ is a decision no one but you can make. You need to own the decision. Even if everything in your background makes saying yes to Christ the logical thing to do, you still need to decide for yourself. Just because you and someone else are blood relatives must not in the slightest take away the precious freedom God gave you to say yes or no.

When you do say yes to Jesus, you are also making future choices based on this primary choice. You are choosing to adopt a Christian worldview about all of life. We are now living in a culture that encourages us to think otherwise. Who would want to eat in a restaurant with only two choices on the menu? And don't the movie theaters nowadays have more than one ... more than six or ten ... how about thirty choices of films? A movie house, which had been showing ten films at once near my home, is now closed. Maybe it did not offer enough choices, as the new theaters do.

One highlight of a trip to the Holy Land is a visit to the top of Mt. Carmel. It was the site where the prophet Elijah challenged the people of God to make up their minds about God. He asked, "How long will you waver between two opinions? If the Lord is God then follow Him; but if Baal, then follow him" (1 Kings 18:21). Then he carried out that famous contest between himself and the prophets of Baal. Elijah prayed and God answered by consuming the animal sacrifice with supernatural fire, proving that He alone is God. This is the kind of challenge God is always making: the either-or variety. We are for Him or against Him. Neutrality has never been an option.

The problem with buying into the pluralist mentality is that all choices about God are not equally good. If all religions are equally good, then none of them is. Honest comparison reveals incompatible beliefs. Truth has the quality of correctness about it. The fact that the claims of Christ are so unique and exclusive is the same reason that they are so *inclusive*. This is because Jesus is everybody's Christ. He is the Savior of all mankind.

The fact is that the truth of Christ is forever valid, regardless of whether or not we choose it or like it. We live in a time when pluralism has led us to believe that spiritual laws apply only to those who want to live under them. Not so. God gives us complete freedom to say yes or no to Him, but not the freedom to be exempt from the consequences of that choice. The truth of God is revealed in Scripture and supremely by Jesus Christ as descriptive of how things are. God's truth is like gravity. People lived with the law of gravity long before Sir Isaac Newton discovered it and taught about it. You do not have to have heard of Isaac Newton or believe his theories to be subject to the law of gravity that God installed at creation. Try jumping out of a window. Your beliefs about Newton will make no difference whatsoever. Gravity does not depend on your knowing about it or accepting it. In the same way, the truth about Jesus Christ does not depend on either your knowing what it is or agreeing to it.

So in this saying, Jesus is telling us that while we have freedom to say yes or no to him, we do not have freedom to complain about the consequences of our choices. He gives us the privilege of the pain of making such false choices, hoping that perhaps we will learn from them. But why learn the hard way? Why not believe that when Jesus says that he has the secret of a truly fulfilling life he is absolutely right! Let's learn to doubt the claims of pluralism, however popular they may be, and believe in the one way God designed us to live. Forget being politically correct or culturally correct. Let's be spiritually correct!

This saying of Jesus reminds us there is a price, a cost, to following him; and that the price can be steep. It requires putting him first, even if it strains the relationship we have with friends and family. We will want to do that when we realize that calling Jesus Lord means letting him *be* Lord. It has been said, "The entrance fee to the Christian life is nothing at all, but the annual subscription is everything you've got." In these puzzling words about a sword, Jesus is saying that he wants us to make a choice. It is a choice no one can make for us, but once we have made it, every other area of our lives is affected and changed for the better.

He Came to Bring Light

"I have come into the world as a light, so that no one who believes in me should stay in darkness" (John 12:46).

We have all had the experience of coming in from a bright outdoors into a restaurant where the atmosphere calls for dim lighting. For a few moments we can barely see where we are going. We sit at a table and strain to read the menu. But before very long our eyes get adjusted to the low level of light and we are comfortable with it. Then, after the meal, we go out into the bright sunshine again and our eyes have to adjust again. Only then do we realize how dark it was inside the restaurant.

In many ways people have a tendency to adjust to a low level of spiritual light and get comfortable with it. We can get so accustomed to hearing about crime, corruption, falsehood and lack of morality that we become calloused and desensitized in our conscience. We think that the problems are too complicated to solve and so we are apt to just settle for the status quo. We get used to the darkness.

Jesus came to show us just how far people had allowed themselves to become accustomed to the darkness of our world. A major theme of the ministry of Jesus is that of light. He was born to lighten up our lives so that we can see God, our world and ourselves as they were meant to be. It is not coincidental that we celebrate Christmas by all sorts of light displays. Christmas decoration involves the use of many colored lights both outside on our homes or lawns and inside on the trees we carry into our living rooms. The symbolism is unmistakable although not everyone makes the connection. Jesus came into the world to light up the darkness of our lives with the truth of God.

Some forty years ago a new church was planned for the Christian community in the city of Nazareth in Israel. The architects decided to make the exterior of the Church of the Annunciation resemble a lighthouse. From any angle of viewing, the tall dome on the limestone brings to mind a key teaching of Jesus: "I am the light of the world. Whoever follows me will never walk in darkness but will have the light of life" (John 8:12). The building preaches a sermon by its very shape. The message is that Jesus is to us what a lighthouse is to a ship. He is the light pointing out dangerous reefs and rocks against which a human life, like a ship, might be dashed to pieces. He is the light we need to plot our position and direction in life so that we can navigate safely through the years to our ultimate destination in heaven.

This is why John uses the image of light to describe the coming of Jesus into the world. "In him was life and that life was the light of men. The light shines in the darkness but the darkness has not understood it" (John 1:5). Another version reads, "has not overcome it" (RSV). In a letter this same author wrote: "This is the message we have heard from him and declare to you: God is light; in him there is no darkness at all" (I John 1:5).

Here is a word picture we can readily grasp. It means that human beings are created to be as dependent on the light of God's truth as the earth is dependent on the light of the sun. Just as God created the sun to dispel the darkness and sustain all living things, so Jesus came to enlighten us with the truth we need to pierce the fog of uncertainty, confusion, and indecision. We need the guidance of Christ to make difficult choices without losing sight of correct values and priorities.

Jesus made his claim to be the light of the world in the context of a worship service in the Jerusalem temple. It was during the Feast of Tabernacles, a time when people came together to celebrate the memory of God's supernatural guidance of the Israelites after they were freed from slavery in Egypt. According to the book of Exodus, God guided them with a pillar of cloud during the day and a pillar of fire during the night. To commemorate this supernatural sign of God's guidance, four large candelabra were placed in the center of an inside courtyard. Then, at a given moment, the candelabra were set ablaze as a dramatic reminder of God's continual guidance during the time of the Exodus wanderings. The people would sing psalms of praise to God for always being to them a light in their darkness.

Imagine for a moment that you were there at that dramatic moment when Jesus of Nazareth walked out into the center of that courtyard near the blazing candelabra and announced in a loud voice, "I am the light of the world." Everyone would have caught the implications of what he was saying. It was as if he said, "God was like light in the darkness for Moses and our ancestors. These great candelabras will soon be put out, but the light that I was born to bring will never be put out because it cannot be put out! I am the light of God which lights up every human being to show the path to everlasting life."

Jesus was teaching that he came into the world to do for us what light does to darkness. He illuminates, he guides, he steers us around obstacles. He penetrates our minds and wills and emotions as we allow him to be our "wonderful counselor." He shines his light into the dark recesses of our soul and exposes things we would rather not see. Nothing remains hidden from him; although there is much about ourselves we prefer not to see. That is why walking in his light requires that we have the courage to want to see what he sees and nothing less. Only if we believe that he comes to cleanse and forgive will we dare to do it.

Jesus said, "This is the verdict: Light has come into the world but men loved darkness instead of light because their deeds were evil. Everyone who does evil hates the light and will not come into the light for fear that his deeds will be exposed. But whoever lives by the truth comes into the light, so that it may be seen plainly that what he has done has been done through God" (John 3:19-21).

What that means is that the light Christ came to bring is not some answer we get simply by going to him in the hour of indecision. Clearly Jesus is saying that his guidance comes not from a certain prayer but from a certain relationship. He says it is a matter of following him and living by the truth. Both verbs imply that obedience and companionship. Seeking God's will only in a crisis hour merely indicates that we have not been walking close to him the rest of the time. If we have been walking in the light we should almost know intuitively what He wants us to do.

Jesus not only said that he was the light of the world but, paradoxically, that every Christian is the light of the world as well. "You are the light of the world. A city on a hill cannot be hidden. Neither do people light a lamp and put it under a bowl. Instead they put it on its stand, and it gives light to everyone in the house. In the same way let your light shine before men, that they may see your good deeds and praise your Father in heaven" (Matt. 5:14-16).

Jesus is the source of the light and we are to be, so to speak, like mirrors reflecting that light into the darkness of our world around us. What Jesus asks is that we do this as faithfully as the moon reflects the light of the sun. We can choose to do either of two things. We can hide our identity as Christians and find plausible excuses for remaining silent about what makes us different from the crowd. Our other option is to act in such a way that people cannot help but wonder what motivates our good deeds. Doing good deeds is not to get anything from God but simply to thank Him for lighting our darkness and erasing our sin debt. If we do this humbly and with a contagious sense of satisfaction and joy, others too will want to know how to experience the light of Christ.

Here is how Peter put it: "Always be prepared to give an answer to everyone who asks you to give a reason for the hope that you have. But do this with gentleness and respect" (I Peter 3:15).

King Solomon lived centuries before Christmas and never knew Jesus, the light of the world. But I have always believed that in his book of Proverbs he gave us the secret of being open and receptive to the light which God would one day send into the world at Christmas. "Trust in the Lord with all your heart and lean not on your own understanding; in all your ways acknowledge him and he will make your paths straight" (Proverbs 3:5,6).

Jesus was born at Christmas not to become the great expert on spiritual things. He came to be for us the one who, because he is God, can enlighten us with the truth so as to make right choices about all things. What a wonderful counselor is Jesus, the light of the world!

He Came To Fulfill the Law and the Prophets

"Do not think that I have come to abolish the Law or the Prophets; I have not come to abolish them but to fulfill them" (Matt. 5:17).

In my college days I took a course in physical education that was an introduction to archery. All of us in the class were untrained in such an ancient sport, but to many of us it seemed an easy way to meet a requirement.

I have forgotten much of what various teachers and professors have said, but, oddly enough, I remember very clearly what the archery instructor told us early in the course. As we bent our bows and pulled back the arrow we heard these words: "Remember, if you aim at the bull's eye you will surely miss it!"

By that the instructor meant that the archer needs to compensate for the downward pull of gravity on the flying arrow. If the arrow is aimed at the bull's eye, gravity's pull during flight will bring it down to a lower circle on the target.

There is also a spiritual principle working in our lives along similar lines. We always have to compensate for the downward pull of our selfish nature. That is why, although we will never actually hit moral and spiritual bull's eyes, we will score higher by aiming higher.

I believe that this is why God laid down standards for human behavior which he knew that we, as fallen human beings, could never actually maintain. But that was no reason to make them easier. In fact, when you read Jesus' own interpretation of the law in His Sermon on the Mount, you find that he actually internalized them all and made them much harder to keep. He focused not on the letter of the law as did the scribes and Pharisees, but on the essence and spirit of the law. He showed us a lived-out example of how God originally intended for people to behave. He fulfilled the law, and in so doing, showed us that these rules for living were timelessly true and relevant.

We live in a time when it is out of fashion to think of God as laying down rules for living that are not negotiable or flexible. That is because absolute authority, even coming from Almighty God, is thought to be unnecessary and old fashioned. Our culture prefers to think that it is nobler to make up our own standards as well as our own truth. What we do not realize is that God never gave us that right or that ability. What we need to see is that those Ten Commandments were never given to take away either our freedom or our enjoyment of God's creation, but rather to protect them. The laws of God, interpreted later by the prophets and finally by Jesus, are like the yellow line in the middle of the highway. In no wise do I feel that being confined to the right side of that line is restrictive. On the contrary, I realize that staying to the right of that line is designed to keep me safe and protect my life.

Recently I had copies of the Ten Commandments framed so that I could arrange for each classroom at the day school of our parish church to post them on the wall. While this is not possible in our public schools, it is still legal in private and parochial schools. The fact remains that even if the children learn the commandments and what they mean, they will still face the great challenge of keeping them. But at least they will know about aiming high and hitting high. This is why James, in his letter, spoke of knowing and obeying the commandments as being similar to looking in a dressing mirror to see what he needs to do to be presentable.

"Anyone who listens to the word but does not do what it says is like a man who looks at his face in a mirror and after looking at himself, goes away and immediately forgets what he looks like. But the man who looks intently in the perfect law that gives freedom, and continues to do this, not forgetting what he has heard but doing it...he will be blessed in what he does" (James 1:23-25).

James is right. You cannot see a dirty face except by looking in a mirror and cleaning it up. Likewise, if you do not know the boundaries of the playing field for life set by the Author of life, how will you know when you are out of bounds? Athletes should be our models. No one has ever tried to make the football field shorter or narrower. It is a game that can be played only as all the players agree to the rules and play by them. No one is allowed to modify them or make them easier. If that happened the game would lose its meaning and its challenge.

In the same way you and I are to accept the laws of God as being timelessly true and necessary for keeping on track morally and spiritually. The fact that we so often fail should have the salutary effect of driving us to our knees. There we are to repent for our breaking of God's laws and humbly ask for the forgiveness He is ready to give. The angel Gabriel was absolutely right. The Savior was born. It was and is good news of great joy that has come to all the people.

He Came to Give Us Life in All Its Fullness
"I have come that they may have life, and have it to the full" (John 10:10).

"There's got to be more to life than this!" Too often we hear people speak this way as they express their disillusionment with life as defined by the culture in which we live. Personally, I feel that God often uses such feelings to cause us to re-examine what it is that we want out of life. Most of the struggles we face are, I believe, rooted in some false understanding of what life is supposed to mean. We too easily accept untruths and illusions about where to find happiness and pursue them as if they were genuine. The result is disappointment, boredom, and disillusionment. But this is actually a blessing! To be set free from anything that misrepresents what God intended for us is a good thing. He wants us to discover the emptiness of life on the world's terms. Then we are ready to revise our thinking and discover that He alone can show us where to find the satisfaction we have been missing.

I love the story that makes this point humorously. One day a man went to his friend who was a farmer. This farmer had been shooting at his barn door for target practice. To his friend's amazement, every bullet hole was in the center of the bull's eye. The man had shot at ten different targets and there were ten holes in the middle of the bull's eye of each of the ten targets.

He said to his friend, "You are amazing! What accuracy! How did you learn to shoot so straight? Have you ever thought about professional matches?"

The friend said, "No, you don't understand. You see, I shoot the bullets first. Then I draw the bull's eyes around the holes!"

We have the American right to pursue happiness, of course, but happiness is not for us to define any way we want. Life is like a coin. We can spend it any way we want, but we can spend it only once. How sad that we can very easily take our cues from the culture and learn the hard way that we are just drawing targets around our own bullet holes.

Jesus came to show us what the Author of life truly had in mind. Jesus called the life God intended us to have "eternal life." "This is eternal life, that they may know **you** the only true God and Jesus Christ whom you have sent" (John 17:3). It is relating to God as we would relate to a close friend. It is not knowing an idea but a person. That means relating to that person. Note also the present tense of the verb. It means that we can relate to God now, this side of heaven.

There are several obstacles that we need to remove if we are to have this kind of relationship with God. One obstacle is acting on the wrong assumption that information and ideas form the basis for knowing God. The age of the computer has truly arrived. Information technology can put a world of facts and data at our fingertips. I am constantly amazed by how this machine can sort, retrieve, organize and analyze data. But even if we had medical, financial, vocational and biographical data about a person, all we would have is a profile on paper. What is required is trust. That comes only as we share with this friend the traits of personality and character that are known only as we choose to reveal them in relationship as friends.

The Bible says that God has already taken the initiative in knowing us. "Before I formed you in the womb I knew you, before you were born I set you apart" God said to Jeremiah (Jer. 1:5). Jesus said to his disciples, "I have called you friends, for everything I have learned from my Father I have made known to you. You did not choose me but I chose you..." (John 15:16). John wrote, "We love because he first loved us" (1 John 4:19). The fact is that God already knows us better than we know ourselves. It is comforting to realize that in spite of what we might like to hide, He wants to be known and loved. That is why he came to seek us out and make the relationship possible.

The first step in knowing God is to make sure we have Him as God. Those who know God, Jesus said, know Him as the only true God. The key is the word *only*. We cannot know God as just one more aim in life, but as the one central aim in life around which all other aims are focused. The first and great commandment is to love God totally, with all our heart, soul, mind and strength (Deut. 6:4). It is what the psalmist meant when he talked about thirsting for God. "As the deer pants for streams of water, so my soul pants for you, O God. My soul thirsts for God, for the living God" (Psalm 42:1,2). We cannot expect to know God as we ought unless we want this relationship with God more than we want anything from Him. I like the way Jeremiah put it. "This is what the Lord says: 'Let not the wise man boast of his wisdom or the strong man boast of his strength or the rich man boast of his riches, but let him who boasts boast about this: that he understands and knows me, that I am the Lord, who exercises kindness, justice and righteousness on earth, for in these I delight,' declares the Lord" (Jer. 9:23,24).

Knowing God begins with deciding that He will be that important to us that He will be our pride and joy. This can happen only as we begin to make His cause ours. We do not pick friends who have radically different aims and values in life. So it is with God. Our relationship with Him will grow as we identify with His cause and stand for His truth. We are to delight in what He delights in, namely kindness, justice and righteousness on the earth.

How do we do this? There are two ways: by letter and by phone. The Lord God has written an open letter to everyone who wants to know Him. I am speaking, of course, about the Bible. There we find everything we need to know God better — advice to take, commands to follow, promises to claim, warnings to heed and examples to follow. The Bible describes itself as a kind of food without which we starve, a sword of faith without which we are defeated, a mirror without which we do not see ourselves as we really are, and a lamp without which we cannot see the path. The apostle Paul wrote "all Scripture is useful for teaching, correcting, rebuking, for training in righteousness, so that the man of God may be thoroughly equipped for every good work" (2 Tim. 3:16). But it does not happen automatically. It requires that we set aside time in our busy lives for meditation on the word of God, and time for contemplating the truth that He is actually present in our midst.

The other way we relate to God is the telephone of prayer. When Jesus taught his disciples to pray he said that they should address God as their Father. Everything about prayer is relational.

If you have caller ID on your phone, you learn the identity of the caller as the telephone rings. If it is the name of a friend you are happy to answer. But what if the name is "Leak-proof Roofing Co."? You are not so apt to answer. Relationship is what gives meaning to any communication. We will want to pray when we realize our heavenly Father is expecting a call. Sometimes it is said that God has a telephone number. His line is never busy. The number is Jeremiah 33:3: "Call me and I will answer you...."

Is there any right way to do it? No, the right way is to begin talking in a conversational way. Ask a parent if there is a right way for a child to call home from camp or from college. Children are welcome to call day or night, whether they are facing a crisis or have nothing much that is going on. So it is with God. He loves to hear from us at any time and any place about anything that is on our mind. The apostle John wrote in one of his letters: "How great is the love the Father has lavished on us that we should be called children of God. And that is what we are" (1 John 3:1).

Knowing God through Jesus Christ in this relational way is what enables us to have life in all its fullness. In fact, once we do know God relationally, it makes whatever else was important to us pale by comparison. Before Paul became a Christian he had everything anyone could want. He had wealth, elite family background, the best of education, a prominent position as a Bible scholar and Pharisee, even membership on the high court known as the Sanhedrin. But he could not say that he knew God in a relational way. But after he gave himself to the risen Christ, everything changed. He became a new person with a totally new understanding of God. Here is how he described the difference:

"But whatever was to my profit I now consider loss for the sake of Christ. What is more, I consider everything a loss compared to the surpassing greatness of knowing Christ Jesus my Lord, for whose sake I have lost all things. I consider them rubbish, that I may gain Christ and be found in him..." (Phil. 3:7-9).

In Trinity Episcopal Church, Boston, you will see just outside the sanctuary a life-sized statue of the famous rector, Phillips Brooks, who served that congregation in the late 19th century. For me it is a sermon in bronze. The great preacher stands at a pulpit with an open Bible. Behind him stands the figure of Jesus whose hand is on Brooks' shoulder. In that statue, I believe, you learn the message of Brooks' greatness. In one of Brooks' letters to a friend he wrote, "All experience comes to be but more and more the pressure of Christ's life upon us. I cannot tell how personal this grows to me. He is here. He knows me and I know Him. It is no figure of speech; it is the reallest thing in the world." [15] Brooks was right. Knowing God as the only true God as we see Him revealed in Jesus Christ whom He sent is indeed life in all its fullness. It is the reallest thing in the world, and it can be ours as well.

Photo by David Livingston

Phillips Brooks, his hand on the Bible,
and the figure of Christ behind him.

Chapter Six

The Characters in the Story

Zechariah and Elizabeth

The story of Jesus actually begins earlier with the birth of a cousin we know as "John the Baptist." John's parents were an elderly couple named Zechariah and Elizabeth, and it is from their experience that we can learn much about praying even when it seems to us that God is not listening.

Zechariah qualified to be a priest in the Jerusalem temple because he was a direct descendant of Aaron, brother of Moses. This was one official calling that was passed on by inheritance from generation to generation. Priests also had to marry women who had a pure Jewish lineage, and if possible, descendants of Aaron. Elizabeth, wife of Zechariah, had such an ideal background.

Zechariah and Elizabeth lived by all the rules, and wanted nothing more than to please God in every thing they did. "Both of them were upright in the sight of God, observing all the Lord's commandments and regulations blamelessly. But they had no children, because Elizabeth was barren, and they were both well along in years" (Luke 1:6).

How much feeling is conveyed by the little word "but." Being childless was tragic for a Jewish couple. Many times this godly family prayed together for a baby as the years of child bearing went by. How their sensitive consciences must have made them wonder why less deserving parents were able to have a family but they were not.

Yet this couple knew that they were to love and serve God because He is God, and not because they wanted something from Him. The relationship with Him is what prayer sustains. Zechariah loved God for who He is, not for what He did or did not grant in answer to prayer. God is not a blessing machine. If we had our prayers answered without getting closer to Him, we would be worse off, not better. God would be no more to us than a kind of genie in a bottle who grants us wishes.

One day Zechariah was given a great privilege, one which came only once in a priest's lifetime, and that only by the luck of the draw. He was chosen that day to go into the inner part of the Temple to burn incense at worship. Many priests were never chosen and Zechariah must have felt closer to God that day than he ever dreamed.

While Zechariah raised his hands and closed his eyes and offered the prayers for the people, God was preparing a great surprise. Imagine the shock when Zechariah opened his eyes and saw an angel in front of him! It was the angel Gabriel who said that he was sent from God to tell him that his prayer had been answered. No doubt Zechariah wondered, "Which prayer?" He had long since given up praying for a child. Maybe the angel meant one of the prayers Zechariah had offered on behalf of the people.

No, the angel Gabriel explained. "Your wife Elizabeth will bear you a son, and you are to give him the name John. He will be a joy and delight to you and many will rejoice because of his birth…" (Luke 1:13). Gabriel went on to tell Zechariah about the future of this baby, that he would be filled with the Spirit of God from his birth, and that his ministry would be one of bringing people back to the Lord so as to be ready for what He would do next.

Zechariah seemed to forget that God is not limited to what seems possible. He asked, "How can I be sure of this? I am an old man and my wife is well along in years" (Luke 1:18). The angel Gabriel answered with what sounds like a tone of rebuke, implying that Zechariah forgot who was speaking. "I am Gabriel, and I stand in the presence of God, and I have been sent to speak to you and to tell you this good news. And now you will be silent and not able to speak until the day this happens, because you did not believe my words, which will come true at their proper time" (Luke 1:19,20).

This was not so much a punishment as it was a constant reminder to Zechariah to trust the power of God more than reason and experience. We can learn from this episode that trust in God does not require full understanding. What is usual and logical is no boundary that limits the limitless power of God.

We also see here the lesson that God does not forget our prayers. It is a mistake to consider that when God says "no" He also means "never." God is weaving together events and circumstances in a mysterious way we do not understand, and His timing is not always ours.

We also see here that we should never conclude that our best days are behind us. Rarely do we imagine that very much of significance will happen after age sixty-five. But the lesson is that we never know. Everything in the past may be preparation for a significant happening we could never have anticipated. For Zechariah and Elizabeth, it was almost like the experience God gave to a very elderly couple named

Abraham and Sarah. They had become parents after they had not only become senior citizens but elderly and aged as well. Zechariah must have known that, but when it came to having babies he trusted in logic and ordinary human experience. This time he was wrong.

The nine months of Zechariah's silence ended when the baby was born. That was when Elizabeth's neighbors and relatives heard that the Lord had shown her great mercy and "they shared her joy" (Luke 1:57). No doubt she told them that what had happened was a miracle, a direct act of God, and that it must mean that God had great plans for her family. She gave the child the name selected by the angel: John, meaning "the Lord's gift."

But naming the child John caused some gossip among the neighbors. "The neighbors were all filled with awe and throughout the hill country of Judea people were talking about these things" (Luke 1:65). What things? It was the fact that an elderly couple had a baby. It was the fact that Zechariah lost his voice and suddenly got it back when the baby was eight days old. And it was the name John. Did that mean he would be somebody special later in life?

"Everyone who heard this wondered about it, asking, 'What then is this child going to be? For the Lord's hand was with him' " (Luke 1:66). We know who the child became. He was the "front man" who got people ready to hear Jesus by preaching to them and leading them to repent and recommit themselves to God in baptism. His name was John and he was the forerunner of Jesus. And he was the man to whom Jesus paid the finest tribute any man has ever received. Jesus said of John, "I tell you, among those born of women there is no one greater than John" (Luke 7:28).

Caesar Augustus

Caesar Augustus was the most powerful person on earth. He was a pagan through and through and believed in many gods. This posed no problem for the God of heaven and earth who used this emperor to fulfill a prophecy about the place of Jesus' birth. Caesar set the story in motion by ordering the empire-wide census.

Augustus was his title. His real name was Octavian, and he was the grandnephew of Julius Caesar. He ruled Rome from 27 BC to 14 AD and was responsible for the time of peace in the empire we know as the Pax Romana. Every fourteen years the Romans took a census, not unlike the census we take in America every ten years. The purpose of the Roman census was for taxation and also for compulsory military service. The Roman government expected complete compliance.

Caesar Augustus was a powerful military figure that united the empire, built roads and cities. One saying goes that when he came to power Rome was a city of brick but when he left it was a city of marble. In 27 BC the Roman Senate rewarded his leadership by giving him the title *Augustus* which means "consecrated or revered." The Senate also changed the name of the month known as Sextilis and named it August. Did you realize that every time you write an August date you are remembering this Roman emperor? But Caesar Augustus never met Jesus. He died in the year 14 AD (in the year of our Lord) rather than in the year 767 AUC (*ab urbe condita*, "from the beginning of the city"). Christ's coming changed the way the world records time.

Caesar would certainly have been surprised to learn that two millennia later people around the world would be celebrating Christmas. Yet if it had not been for him, there would have been no birth in Bethlehem, no Nativity scene, no shepherds and everything else we associate with the circumstances of Jesus' birth. God can and does use anyone and everyone, including those who do not believe in Him, to accomplish His purpose.

Unfortunately, the popularity Caesar enjoyed led many to think he was a god himself. Some later emperors actually thought of themselves as gods and required the Roman people to worship them. Nevertheless, Caesar Augustus lived in a time much like ours when people believe that there are many equally good spiritual choices and many paths that are available. Caesar worshipped many pagan gods and never understood why the Jews would worship only one. His viewpoint has certainly had a revival in our time.

Many people today think that way. Religion, for them, is like a tool to use to get favors from God. It is not a faith that controls them but a faith that they control. Since they cannot manipulate God or ingratiate themselves with Him to ask favors, this kind of distorted faith will never satisfy. In fact it is a form of idolatry. Faith in God is not about earning or deserving God's favor. It is about accepting the gift of forgiveness through what Christ did on the cross, and then, in gratitude, giving him permission to be Master and Lord.

Caesar Augustus also reminds me that while he could demand that a census be taken throughout his empire and everyone would have to obey, God never issues any such decree. Surely Luke saw that contrast. Consider the decree that went out from God. It was not a decree ordering something to happen, but rather a news bulletin delivered not to everyone in the empire, but only to some humble shepherds near Bethlehem. Moreover, the message of the angels was puzzling. They were told of a baby being born who would be Christ the Lord, and that this baby would be found in the most unlikely place, not in a palace but in a stable and in a manger. And yet, oddly, this baby was going to bring joy to all the people.

Looking back over the years, Luke could not have missed this stark contrast between the way Caesar ruled and the way God ruled. Caesar ruled by military power; God ruled in humility. Caesar gave people no choice but to obey. "All the world went to be enrolled, each to his own city." But not so with God. His way was the way of invitation and free choice. God's decree was that everyone should be offered a gift. "God so loved the world that he gave his only begotten Son, that whoever believes in him should not perish but have everlasting life" (John 3:16).

Herod the King

Herod was the puppet "king of the Jews," set up and handled by his emperor Augustus Caesar. He came to power only because of his father's friendly ties with Augustus. Once he was in power he decided to leave a legacy of magnificent buildings, palaces, aqueducts and entire cities such as Caesarea with its impressive port. However, because of his lack of genuine faith in God, he saw nothing wrong with a more pluralistic approach to governing. He erected temples to pagan deities. He would have said that his greatest building project was the restoration and extension of the temple in Jerusalem. It was a truly magnificent building project.

Politically he was astute. In a depressed economy he would remit the taxes but most of the time he taxed the people cruelly. Before long he was so obsessed with his own greatness and power that he began to be suspicious of everyone. We might understand a king being worried about armies approaching his borders or about discovering a plot by assassins who want to kill him. Imagine, then, how odd it was for a

73-year-old king to feel threatened by the birth of a baby to a poor carpenter and his wife. He was so paranoid and insecure on hearing about a newborn king that he thought it wise to murder all babies in Bethlehem two years old and under. This was not surprising for a man of his character. He ruled as a ruthless and jealous tyrant. His lust for power consumed him. He distrusted everyone, even those in his family. He killed his brothers and half-brothers, two sons and his own wife, all in an attempt to feel more secure on his throne.

This background explains his deceiving the wise men by saying they were to locate the child and let him know about it. But when the wise men, warned by an angel about Herod's trickery, went back another way, Herod was livid. He ordered the slaughter of the babies in Bethlehem. What did he care? Had you asked, he would have replied, "I did what I had to do. I was only protecting my throne." But his plan backfired because though he did not know it he was fighting against Almighty God.

When Herod was old and ill, he knew people would not mourn but rather rejoice at his death. So he concocted a plan to guarantee that on the day he died there would be public mourning. Leaders from all over Judea were to be locked up inside the great hippodrome in Jericho where he had a palace. On his death these people were to be murdered so that there would be a widespread feeling of sadness on the day he died. Fortunately, his plan failed and Herod's order was never carried out. Those earmarked for death were set free.

The baby who eluded Herod's holocaust was safe with his mother and stepfather in the land of Egypt. After Herod was dead the angel notified Joseph and Mary in a dream that it was now safe to return. But Herod's son Archelaus was ruling in Herod's place and he was just as cruel and tyrannical. The angel warned them not to go there. So they did not return to Judea but went back north to Galilee and their former home in Nazareth where they could have some semblance of a normal family life.

What can this sad story of a ruthless and cruel king teach us? It can remind us that Herod and Jesus could not coexist. One of them had to go. Herod made his decision and tried his best to stop Jesus. He failed because he set himself against God. For us it means that we are confronted with a similar decision placed before us by God. Either we are for Jesus or we are against him. There is no middle ground of indifferent neutrality. Neutrality is actually a subtle form of opposition. That is why those who want to go their own way are troubled by the message of Jesus. They like to think they are on the right track but the gospel of Jesus Christ says that they are foolish people headed only for great sorrow and disappointment.

Let us realize that God would not have bothered to come into our world as He did and suffer for our sins on the cross if there had been some better way. As we celebrate each Christmas, let it be for us a time of agreeing with God about our need for a Savior, and of making sure that we have consciously and deliberately decided to follow him.

Joseph

"Is not this the carpenter's son? Is not his mother called Mary?" (Matt. 13:55)

Who was Joseph? If you think of the Christmas nativity scene you can picture him standing there beside Mary as both are looking into the face of the baby Jesus. But we know very little about Joseph, the foster father of Jesus. We do know that he was a devout and orthodox Jewish man, and that he was a "just" man, a word that suggests that he tried sincerely to live an upright, virtuous, God-pleasing life. It is a word used in the Bible to describe Noah (Gen. 6:9), Lot (2 Peter 2:6), John the Baptizer (Mark 6:20) and Cornelius (Acts 10:22). A righteous or just person is one who conscientiously serves God. He is someone who tries his best always to do what is right.

Joseph is the quiet one in the Christmas story. He is spoken about and spoken to but he never speaks in the story. He is a supporting actor. While we have no words from him, his actions speak volumes. He is an important figure in the story by means of what God said to him and did through him. Here we see a man of deep faith, raw courage, and steadfast obedience to the will of God. God spoke to him in dreams no less than four times. In those dreams, we learn that Joseph has a vital role to play in caring for and protecting Mary and the newborn Savior of the world.

God spoke to Joseph in the first dream when he and Mary were engaged. Young girls would marry as teenagers in that culture, whereas men would usually wait until their mid twenties. Parents arranged marriages for the most part, but parents would certainly consider the comments and behavior of their children in deciding which family to contact. Love was truly a factor as well. However, orthodox Jewish families tried very hard not to leave such an important matter as marriage to the feelings of their children. Joseph and Mary may well have been picked out for each other by the two sets of parents even before the couple met.

When the legal engagement began, there was a formal prayer over the couple as they tasted a cup of wine together, and the fathers agreed to the marriage contract. Then the couple would wait a full year during which they were regarded as husband and wife, but they did not live together. There was no sexual union until the actual wedding ceremony. Though Joseph and Mary were engaged, a formal divorce would be required to end the engagement. Had either party been unfaithful it would be considered adultery, and had Joseph died during the engagement Mary would have been considered a widow.

We can only imagine the shock and embarrassment Joseph felt upon learning that Mary was expecting a baby. Mary had been gone for three months visiting her cousin Elizabeth and now she is pregnant. We do not know how he learned of it. But you can guess what questions raced through his mind. Who is the father? When and where and why did this happen? Surely Joseph felt the sting of betrayal from the woman he dearly loved. We can hardly imagine how devastated he must have been.

Joseph, of course, did nothing wrong. Yet even after he discovered that Mary was pregnant he did not react out of anger, but out of compassion and love. "Because Joseph her husband was a righteous man and did not want to expose her to public disgrace, he had in mind to divorce her quietly" (Matt. 1:19). What that reveals to us is that Joseph based his decision not on circumstances but upon his own character. He would treat Mary kindly even though it appeared that she had betrayed him.

All of us face situations not of our own making; when someone else does something that completely changes our lives. Things happen over which we have no control and they affect our lives as a result. Maybe it is a reckless driver who causes an accident that leaves us seriously injured. Maybe it is an employer who decides that our whole department is going to be laid off. Maybe it is a financial advisor we trusted but who invested our savings unwisely. How will we respond? We may, like Joseph, not have all the facts we need to make a good decision. We cannot wait until we have all the information we want. Yet we have to do something. This is the time for us to do what Joseph did — to base our decision not on information or the lack thereof, but on the content of our character and the kind of persons we are.

This is what Joseph did. He pondered three options open to him. He could marry Mary immediately and hope that the neighbors would not gossip too much about a baby born in six months. He could publicly denounce Mary as an adulteress, which would lead to her death by stoning. Or he could send her away to another town where she was not known, have the marriage contract voided, and let her have the baby. The last option seemed the right thing to do.

We need to note here that Joseph had made up his mind about what to do before the angel came and explained what really had happened. "But after he had considered this, an angel of the Lord appeared to him in a dream and said, 'Joseph, son of David, do not be afraid to take Mary home as your wife, because what is conceived in her is from the Holy Spirit. She will give birth to a son, and you are to give him the name Jesus, because he will save his people from their sins' " (Matt. 1: 20,21).

What good news! Mary is still a virgin! God is the father of the baby, not some other man. But my guess is that after thinking about the dream a while, Joseph heard the voice of doubt in his mind. After all, it was a dream and people dream all sorts of unlikely things. Should he go ahead with marriage plans based on a dream about an angel of God? Suppose there was a more natural explanation and Mary was not a virgin anymore. Joseph had lots of unanswered questions but he had to make a decision.

You and I face times when we have to make a decision without all the information and facts we would like to have. That is when the best thing is to do what Joseph did. He did what was right on the basis of his righteous character and his trust in God. "When Joseph woke up he did what the angel of the Lord commanded and took Mary home as his wife. But he had no union with her until she gave birth to a son. And he gave him the name Jesus" (Matt. 1:24,25).

From the clues we have in the Bible weddings were quite elaborate. There was a procession with musical accompaniment to the place of the wedding. There were attendants on both sides and a feast after the ceremony. Considering the fact that both Joseph and Mary came from rather poor families, this ceremony would have been kept very simple.

What stands out about Joseph being chosen of God to be the husband of Mary and the stepfather of the Christ child is his ordinary station in life. He was a humble working man, someone who cut trees into boards for building materials, walls, beams, yokes, plows and wagons. In our minds he would not be the one we would choose to be the foster father of Jesus. Nor had it ever occurred to him that this would be his lot. He had not volunteered Mary for the role of mother of the Savior.

If you or I had been God we might have made other kinds of choices. We might have chosen to have Jesus born into a family more involved in spiritual things, one of the priestly families at the temple, for example. That sounds like a more logical choice. Instead of poor parents, why not give the Savior a well-to-do upbringing, the best of schools, an introduction into the right social circles? Wouldn't that serve Jesus well later on in his ministry? Being well connected has always opened doors. But God did not think it necessary.

No, what this selection of Joseph and Mary as earthly parents says is that God can use ordinary people to do extraordinary things. Consider who heard the news of Jesus' birth — ordinary shepherds! And they found the Savior not in the palace of Herod, not in the house of Caiaphas the high priest, but in a stable behind an inn, lying in a manger, a trough for feeding animals.

God has a way of surprising us just as He did Joseph. He does it unexpectedly and in unlikely ways with unpredictable results. He will not be confined to our narrow definitions of Him. He will not act according to our expectations of Him. We would do well to ponder the message of God given to the prophet Isaiah: "As the heavens are higher than the earth, so are my ways higher than your ways and my thoughts than your thoughts" (Is. 55:9).

The next time we hear of Joseph he has stepped out of the Nativity scene in which we see him standing next to Mary. After the wise men came with their gifts and went on their way, an angel spoke to Joseph a second time in a dream. This time the angel said, " 'Get up, take the child and his mother and escape to Egypt. Stay there till I tell you, for Herod is going to search for the child to kill him.' So he got up, took the child and his mother during the night and left for Egypt, where he stayed till the death of Herod" (Matt. 2:13, 14).

Under the cover of darkness, Joseph took Mary and Jesus and headed for Egypt. Since the border was not far it was probably not much more than a twenty-four-hour trip, a distance of about sixty miles. Outside of Herod's jurisdiction they would be safe. But the trip across the Sinai sands would be hard. What a sudden change of scenery from the

Bethlehem stable to the lonely road with the wind blowing around them and stinging them with moving sand. Egypt was something like a place of retreat, a neutral country where people could take refuge. How odd that Joseph and Mary and the baby Jesus should become refugees.

What we see here is an obedient Joseph. He did not ask the logical question, "How long do we have to stay there?" Rather, his action of immediately following the angel's direction suggests that Joseph took God at His word, believing that God was going to look after him and Mary and the child, and that He was protecting them fully. Here we see a Joseph who believes God implicitly. He is courageous and willing to tackle the difficult and hazardous journey to Egypt.

What can we learn from Joseph's retreat to Egypt? It reminds us that people are going to take sides when it comes to Jesus Christ. As we saw in our study of why Jesus came, he said that people will either be for or against him, and that this choosing up of sides will happen even in the same family. Herod is, in a real sense, still around. He always has been.

That is why you cannot become a Christian without making changes in your heart and mind and life. The message of Jesus Christ is at odds with the message of the postmodern culture in which we live. That is why those who put their trust in power, popularity, position, possessions, and politics will not be able to hear, let alone subscribe to, the real gospel of Jesus Christ. They are likely to want to have nothing to do with Christians. That is why Herod went even further. He did not just ignore Jesus. He tried to eliminate him. But what he did not know was this: It was a contest between a cruel tyrant and Almighty God. How futile!

The third time the angel spoke to Joseph and said, "Get up, take the child and his mother and go to the land of Israel, for those who were trying to take the child's life are dead"

(Matt. 2:19). It was a message of hope and expectation. It communicated to him the reassurance that God always has the last word and always wins out over any who oppose Him. His will cannot be thwarted. Evil may seem to be on the throne, but it merely appears that way. The God who brought Joseph and Mary and Jesus safely from Bethlehem to refuge in Egypt can also be trusted to protect and provide for us whatever comes along. We are told that Joseph followed the directions of the angel and went back to Israel.

Then the angel spoke a fourth time and warned Joseph about Herod's son Archelaus reigning in Judea. So Joseph continued north to Galilee and to the village of Nazareth, where both he and Mary had been raised.

Nazareth was a very ordinary place, a kind of "Nowheresville" of the time. It was a backwater place that no one liked. "Can anything good come from Nazareth?" (John 1:46) was the popular expression that would later be spoken to demean Jesus' background. Yet it was there that Jesus spent his childhood years, apprentice to his father in the carpenter's shop.

The last glimpse we get of Joseph is when Jesus got lost at age twelve. After he and Mary left Jerusalem following the Passover celebration, they assumed that Jesus was in the company of relatives traveling with them. They went a whole day's journey before discovering that Jesus was not present. Returning to Jerusalem they found him in the temple having a theological discussion with the learned rabbis. Frustrated and hurt they asked, "Son, why have you treated us like this? Your father and I have been anxiously searching for you."

Jesus replied, "Why were you searching for me? Didn't you know I had to be in my father's house?" Another translation reads, "Did you not know I must be about my Father's business?" (King James Version) The Greek translates literally, "the things of my Father" (Luke 2:48-50).

We do not have any words from Joseph or Mary, just the line that says, "they did not understand what he was saying to them" (Luke 3:50). Every parent of a teenager can relate to that experience! And this is the last reference we have to the foster father of Jesus. We are simply told that the family returned to Nazareth and Jesus "was obedient to them" and that "he grew in wisdom and in stature, in favor with God and man" (Luke 3:52). After this, nothing more is ever said about Joseph, not once during the three year ministry of Jesus. A safe assumption is that at some point Joseph died. Jesus then assumed the burden of being eldest son and providing for his mother, his brothers and sisters. He learned first hand the responsibility of running a small business, keeping records, working long hours at tiring labor, dealing with the public, and allocating income to meet expenses of the family.

Years later, when Jesus began his ministry, he would use a term for God which had not been used before. He said that God is like an understanding, caring father. Can we reasonably assume that Jesus learned about fatherhood from observing it being modeled by his stepfather, Joseph? As the old saying goes, "an apple does not fall far from the tree." The relationship of Joseph and Jesus was so right and so good that Jesus knew that the best way of describing God's love was to refer to it as fatherly. Surely Joseph was at least partly the source of that inspiration.

Joseph and Mary had children of their own after the birth of Jesus. Mark's gospel states clearly states this. When Jesus began his ministry, the people who knew him in the role of carpenter remarked, "Is not this the carpenter, the son of Mary and the brother of James and Joses and Judas and Simon, and are not his sisters here with us?" (Mark 6:3) A similar list appears in Matthew 13:55 with the exception of Joseph for "Joses."

Protestants take these statements literally as being the half-brothers and half-sisters of Jesus. We can also note that Matthew says "Joseph had no union with Mary until she had given birth to a son" (Matt. 1:25). This suggests that their marital relationship was quite normal and produced children conceived and born as any other children are. Also, we find in Luke 2:7 that Mary gave birth to her "firstborn son." The implication is that there were others that followed.

Roman Catholics and Eastern Orthodox Christians, however, insist on the perpetual virginity of Mary. They deal with the above texts by saying that the brothers and sisters refer to children of Joseph by a previous marriage, or perhaps as cousins, or that they were children of another Mary, the wife of Alphaeus, sister of the Virgin Mary. However, these ideas have no Scriptural support.

Mary, the Virgin Mother

What do we know about her? We know little about her background or family except that her father was named Eli (Luke 3:23). The name Mary means "The Lord's beloved."

What we do know by implication is that she must have rated very high with God for Him to select her to bear His son, the Savior. The angel visited her and called her "highly favored." It is a word used only twice in the New Testament, in the annunciation story (Luke 1:28) and again in Ephesians 1: 6 where it is translated "glorious grace."

We wonder what the angel meant by saying that Mary had found favor with God. "Greetings, you who are highly favored (highly graced)" (Luke 1:28). Roman Catholics have a prayer based on the greeting: "Hail Mary, full of grace." In Scripture we read that Noah found grace in the eyes of the Lord. Abraham, Moses, Ruth, David, and others did also. Mary stands in a long line of biblical figures that found grace with God. Grace means God's undeserved love and blessing.

We can well understand Mary's first reaction to the angel's words. "Mary was greatly troubled at his words and wondered what kind of greeting this might be" (Luke 1:29). Anytime someone brings us unexpected announcements there is a sense of foreboding and fear of the unknown. Perhaps it is a bulletin that our company is being merged and we will need to relocate. Perhaps it is a doctor saying that the annual physical revealed something suspicious and there is a need for further examination. It might be a phone call in the middle of the night informing us that a relative is seriously ill.

I am sure that Mary's face revealed this sense of fear. After all, this was not a dream but a wide-awake experience of a supernatural being! As far as we know it was a first-time encounter with an angel. She had the presence of mind to listen and not run and hide. The angel immediately tried to dispel her fear with a word of comfort. The angel said, "Do not be afraid, Mary, you have found favor with God." He then told her what to expect: "You will be with child and give birth to a son, and you are to give him the name Jesus. He will be great and will be called the Son of the Most High. The Lord God will give him the throne of his father David, and he will reign over the house of Jacob forever; his kingdom will never end" (Luke 1:30-33).

Can you imagine trying to process that message? She was told that although she was a virgin she would become pregnant and deliver a baby! Moreover, the baby was no less than the Son of God and would grow up to be king of a never-ending kingdom! It seemed totally impossible! Even if it were going to happen, why would God choose Mary, a teenage girl from a poor family in Nazareth? She must have been wondering if God had sent the angel to the wrong address!

Consider what she must have been thinking. "Why did the angel come to me? What will Joseph say? How will my family and the neighbors react? What will it be like to be the mother of such a unique child? What about my plans to marry and have a family with Joseph? Do I have to do this or is God asking me to pray about it and decide if I really want it?"

All these questions were going through her mind, but one question seemed uppermost: "How will this be, since I am a virgin?" She knew how babies come into the world and that a human father would be needed. The angel answered her question directly and accurately but the answer raised as many questions as it answered. "The Holy Spirit will come upon you, and the power of the Most High will overshadow you. So the holy one to be born will be called the Son of God" (Luke 1:35). As we noted earlier in our study of the virgin birth there is a mystery to the word "overshadow." Perhaps it was the best the angel could do, knowing that Mary or any of us, for that matter, would never be able to understand the method by which God would conceive a child in a human mother.

Then the angel said so much in so few words, "For nothing is impossible with God." Mary was asked to leave all the details to God and simply accept the role she was offered.

Let's not think it was all that easy. Did she say yes because the angel's presence was intimidating? No. I believe that the angel spoke in such a way as to communicate the respect God has for human freedom. She could have said no. God never coerces anybody to do His will.

And let's not minimize the risks of saying yes. How would she explain this to her parents and to her fiancé Joseph? Joseph would have reason to break the engagement. At best she would have been shunned by society and at worst would risk being stoned for adultery. What the angel was calling her to do was to set aside her reason, her experience and her common sense and step into an unknown future with nothing but faith in God. I don't know how long she pondered the choice but she came up with her final answer. "I am the Lord's servant. May it be to me as you have said" (Luke 1:38).

What has always intrigued me about her choice is that she had such little information to go on and that as far as we know she asked only one question. She was, in fact, signing a contract without reading the fine print and without fully understanding what she was consenting to. Such was her trust in God. She believed that God would never ask her to do anything that He would not also equip her to do. She believed that God would never ask of her anything which would not be in her own best interests.

What about us? Does our wanting to know in advance what doing His will requires water down our commitment to God? So often people want to know God's will not because they are anxious to do it, but simply out of curiosity. Then, they reason, they will give it consideration and if it seems good to them they will commit to doing it. Jesus said that it does not work this way. "If anyone chooses to do God's will he will find out whether my teaching comes from God or whether I speak on my own" (John 17:7). The truth is that

God reveals His will to people like Mary who volunteer to be His servants without feeling the need to find out first if they like it.

In various ways you and I are faced with Mary's decision to accept or reject the will of God. What it all comes down to is the question of just how much we trust God. Do we believe that the best choice is always the one God asks us to make? Are we ready to say yes to Him without any strings attached and without fully understanding where the decision will lead?

In addition to the episode where Mary and Joseph look for and find Jesus in the temple at age twelve, there are several other key references to Mary. When Jesus has already begun his ministry we find Mary at a wedding in Cana to which Jesus and his disciples have also been invited (John 2:1-11). Mary apparently has been given a role in hosting the reception. At one point the wine ran out. She decided to tell Jesus about it. "They have no wine!" she said, with a tone of urgency in her voice.

Jesus replied, "Dear woman, why do you involve me? My time has not yet come." He meant by that that he had his "hour" or his mission on his mind and the task of supplying enough wine for a wedding party was not on his agenda.

Mary had to learn that day to release Jesus to be his own person with his own identity, an independent, mature person. Mothering and fathering always means gradually giving a child more and more independence. This is easier said then done, as parents know. But just as toddlers cannot walk without taking the risk of falls, neither can older children enter adulthood until parents release them to assume responsibility for their own future.

Mary needed to release Jesus from her supervision and from taking her orders so that he could get on with his career as Savior of the world. The old saying is true; "If you love something set it free. If it comes back to you than it is yours. If it does not return then it was never yours in the first place."

The next time we meet Mary is in the town of Capernaum, midpoint in Jesus' ministry. He is up against stern opposition from people who claim he is deranged, even de-mon-possessed. His whole family heard about it and made their way to where Jesus was teaching. They passed a note through the crowd that said, "Your mother and brothers and sisters are standing outside, wanting to see you."

He replied, "My mother and brothers are those who hear God's word and put it into practice" (Luke 8:19-21).

Imagine how Mary felt. Did she catch the meaning of what he said? Jesus had come to bring into being a different kind of family where people become brothers and sisters in a different way. They would be bound together not by blood ties but by their common allegiance to him. It is a spiritual family under the headship of Christ. A mother should want her children to take their place in the extended family of Jesus Christ, the Christian Church. It can only happen if the faith in the parents' hearts is so real that the child grows up with a clear picture of what life in that extended family is like.

Jesus' last words to his mother were spoken from the cross. In pain he looked down at his mother watching nearby stand-ing next to his friend John. Note that Joseph is not there. Surely he would have been there had he been alive. Jesus said to Mary, "Woman, behold your son" (John 19:26). He was asking Mary to take care of John and minister to his needs. What this tells us is that the love of a mother (or father) is most mature when it is given where it is most needed, not just where it is expected or reciprocated.

The Shepherds

Prominent in the nativity scene with Joseph, Mary, the baby Jesus and the wise men are shepherds from nearby fields. Having been to "Shepherds' Field" in Bethlehem while hosting pilgrimages to the Holy Land, I can assure you that it is a moving thing to stand there and sing "O Little Town of Bethlehem." Amazingly, shepherds are still there today. They are mostly nomadic Bedouin families living in tents. They see the tourists come and go but otherwise live much as shepherds have always lived since Bible times, watching their flocks, caring for the sheep.

What we do not usually ponder is the fact that God made a strange choice in announcing the birth of the Savior to such people as shepherds. Logic would suggest that God would announce this great event to people of position and prestige, not to those on the fringes of society. If God wanted to let the world know about what He was doing on their behalf, don't you think He would have fared better by starting with people who could help make it known? Why not start with the Roman emperor who already believed in many gods? Let Caesar know that in one of the remote provinces of his empire the God of the Hebrew people has been born of a woman. But would God want the Savior to be thought of by anyone as just one more pagan deity? No. Then how about announcing the birth to those who were expecting the Messiah, namely the religious leaders in Jerusalem? Wouldn't an angelic visitation to the high priest or to the religious leaders of the Sanhedrin give the Christmas story an appropriate beginning? No. The problem was that Jesus had no intention of being the kind of military and political figure that such people were expecting.

Religious people looked down on shepherds. It was not that the work of shepherds was unimportant. They worked hard though they were paid little. The wool of sheep was used for clothing and their meat was widely used as meat. But shepherds could not keep the religious rules about washing and observing the Sabbath. People did not trust them and they became the butt of jokes and undeserved prejudice. Their testimony was not acceptable in a court of law. They suffered from what we call discrimination and segregation.

Even so, shepherding dated way back in Jewish history. The Jews came into the Promised Land not as farmers but as nomadic tribes of shepherds with their herds of sheep. Many references in Scripture apply to sheep and shepherds. As a matter of fact, God chose men who were shepherds and called them to be some of the great patriarchs. Some examples are Abraham, Isaac, Jacob, as well as Moses and David.

Why then do you suppose God chose to announce the birth of the Messiah to these lowly shepherds? Was it to say that the things that impress us did not impress Him? Was it to be a hint that the Messiah would later preach about the shallow pleasures that come from seeking worldly power, fame and wealth? His teachings were in sharp contrast with the definition of success and happiness most people were striving to attain.

Could it also be that God chose the shepherds because the word shepherd best described how Jesus would relate to his people? King David wrote the 23rd Psalm comparing God to a shepherd. Jesus would later say that he was the good shepherd who was going to lay down his life for his sheep. Even in contemporary Christianity the shepherding role is used to define ordained ministry. Clergy are called "pastor" in some denominations. The word "bishop" and "priest" both derive their meaning from New Testament words meaning "overseer" and "shepherd." Perhaps God's choice of the shepherds was deliberate and symbolic.

God's choice may be symbolic in another sense. That is because these shepherds were entrusted with the sheep being raised for sacrifice in the nearby Temple in Jerusalem. There was need for a continuous supply of healthy and unblemished sheep that could pass rigid inspection by the priests at the temple. These sheep were born for sacrifice in Jerusalem. It just might be that this was a subtle symbol of the fact that the child born in Bethlehem was also going to be the perfect and ultimate sacrifice for the sins of mankind in the city of Jerusalem some thirty years later.

Regardless of why, God sent the angels to announce the birth of the Savior to the shepherds keeping watch over their flocks by night. And they heard the message. Not only did they hear it; they actually listened to it. There is a big difference. Most people in America have heard the story of Jesus, at least the gist of it, the part we call "information." That is where faith begins ... getting the facts. Paul asks his friends in the congregation in Rome, "How can they believe in the one of whom they have not heard. Faith comes by hearing the message, and the message is heard through the word of Christ." (See Romans 10:14-17).

Jesus would one day remind his disciples that hearing involves the ears but also the heart. It means listening to what is said and interpreting what is meant. It means being receptive to the information communicated. That is why so many people have heard the old, old story but have never made a commitment to Jesus as Savior and Lord. What we see in the shepherds is that kind of receptivity which is required for genuine faith.

We also see the shepherds doing something everyone in our day needs to do. They went and validated the claims about Jesus. "'Let's go to Bethlehem and see this thing that has happened, which the Lord has told us about.' So they hurried off and found Mary and Joseph and the baby, lying in a manger" (Luke 2:15). There is the secret. It is caring enough about the message to check out the claims people are making about Jesus. Second-hand faith doesn't work. Our pastor, our spouse, our parents, cannot do our believing for us.

Notice also how the shepherds did not procrastinate but hurried off to validate the angels' message. Shepherding is a twenty-four-hours-a-day, seven-days-a-week kind of business. We do not know who they found to look after the sheep while they went to Bethlehem, but they found people to do it. Where there is a will there is a way.

Certainly I am not advising that anyone make a sudden commitment to Christ without first considering carefully what is required. But it is a mistake to procrastinate by first trying to make us more worthy of belonging to Christ. That day will never come. We cannot do anything to make him love us more or to make him love us less. Sam Shoemaker, an Episcopal priest and evangelist of an earlier generation, used to say, "Commit as much of yourself as you know to as much of God as you see revealed in Jesus Christ." This leaves the door open for more growth and understanding of ourselves and also of God. It is a good way of avoiding the temptation to delay. You never know what tomorrow will bring.

Then, also, the shepherds told others about Jesus. "When they had seen Jesus they spread the word concerning what had been told them about the child" (Luke 2:17). What was that? It was that the child would grow up to be the Messiah, the Savior, Christ, the Lord. That was not their opinion. They were merely repeating to other people what God said about Jesus. They might well have been discouraged before they began. They were the least credible witnesses in the community. Who would believe them? And why would anyone be amazed at anything they would say?

I believe it was not just the message they told; it was the nonverbal communication that was most convincing. No doubt as they spread the word about the child born in Bethlehem they met people who knew them. These people noticed the body language of the shepherds, the excitement in their voices, and their courage in wanting to tell of their experience to anyone who would listen. They sensed the obvious difference and this gave weight to their testimony.

That is the calling of every believer. It is to relay to others not our ideas about who we think Jesus is — many have been dead wrong about him. Rather, we are to describe His identity as the shepherds did. He is God in the flesh. "In Christ all the fullness of the deity lives in bodily form," said Paul (Col. 2:9). Had you asked the shepherds, "Are you saying you understand how this baby can be human and also God?" they would have said no. They did not feel they had to comprehend God but simply to relay what God had said about Jesus with the convincing testimony of a changed life.

There is a before and after to every believer's autobiography. Being a faithful follower of Jesus is a matter of show and tell. The changes in our goals, values, priorities and lifestyle combine to make a powerful nonverbal witness. But we also need to give credit where credit is due and point to Jesus as the one who made these changes possible. People are still being amazed and God is still using that amazement to motivate them to want to discover the Savior for themselves.

Last of all, "the shepherds returned, glorifying and praising God for all the things they had heard and seen, which were just as they had been told" (Luke 2:20). That is why Christmas is worth celebrating. When we do it in the right way, we go into every New Year with an increased sense of the trustworthiness of God. He did not mislead the shepherds. It was no joke. They went back to their humdrum job of shepherding with a conviction that God had let them in on a wonderful secret, which would give new hope to everybody. It was a hope so real that life for these shepherds would never be the same. They would live every day in light of that night when the angels gave them the privilege of being the first to know of that great miracle which would literally give time and history a brand new start.

The Wise Men
What an odd collection of people we find in the Christmas card Nativity scenes! No prominent people are there. Caesar Augustus and King Herod are absent. The chief priests and religious leaders are missing. The only visitors are some neighboring shepherds and some Gentile astrologers from Persia known as "wise men," or magi.

Who were the wise men? The Christmas carol begins, "We three kings of Orient are...," but already we see three errors. We do not know how many wise men there were. Traditionally we have assumed there were three because there were three gifts: gold, frankincense and myrrh. Second, we have no reason to think they were kings. And third, they did not come from the Orient (our far East) but simply from "the East." That meant "Middle East" and was no doubt a reference to Persia and Mesopotamia.

The text refers to them as "magi." They were an old and powerful priestly caste among the Persians who lived some 700 miles away in what is modern Iran. They were supposed to be very knowledgeable in medicine, astronomy, and what we would call today the sciences. They were formed in about the sixth century BC in the region of Chaldea (modern Kurdistan.) They were referred to in Daniel 2:2 as Chaldeans.

When Persia conquered Babylon in 538 BC, the various wise men of Babylon were assimilated into Persian culture, and they gradually acquired respect and influence. Often they would roam far from Persia and offer their skills and knowledge to any receptive countries. Their craft was a beef-stew of many arts and practices, ranging from sorcery, astrology, and witchcraft to genuine scientific research. It is not surprising that our word magic derives from the same root. The ancient world made little distinction between astrology and astronomy, between superstition and science, and the magi were experts in all of it. They served as scholars, interpreters of dreams, and legal authorities. Our word *magistrate* is also derived from magi.

It is likely that the wise men were aware of Jewish prophecies about a coming Messiah-king. Centuries earlier, when the Jews were living as captives in Babylon, Daniel managed to be elevated to a position of great honor. The king rewarded Daniel because he had interpreted a dream that the magi of that day could not interpret. Daniel would have been in contact with these magi who served the king with him. Knowing what we do about Daniel's character and his zeal for God, we can be sure that Daniel would have wanted to teach the magi about the identity of the true God. He would have introduced them to the Scripture and the prophecies about a coming Messiah. One of them may have been, "There shall come a star out of Jacob and a scepter shall rise from Israel" (Numbers 24:17).

We cannot tell just how much Old Testament knowledge was assimilated into the magi's background. It is clear, though, that much of it was passed down to the time of Christ. God may well have chosen to set aside and overrule the magi's practice of astrology, and instead direct them by a method consistent with their habit of stargazing. Scholars have debated for centuries whether or not the moving star might have been some comet or a conjunction of the planets Jupiter and Saturn. No one knows. Some scholars have pointed out that because of the rotation of the earth anything in the night sky appears to move westward as the night goes on, and as people travel the stars do seem to move with them and stop when they stop. So the star of Christmas, while a perfectly natural phenomenon, would seem to be stopping for the magi as they reached their destination.

That may be a stretch simply to make the moving star scientifically credible for us moderns. Just as plausible, I think, is the suggestion that it could well have been the kind of moving light Moses was given for the people of Israel as they wandered through the desert. They were literally following a moving pillar of fire by night, and cloud by day. (Exodus 13:21) Who is to say that God could not or would not supply such a moving light to guide the Persian astrologers to the child of Bethlehem?

With the guidance they had, however, still they had no specific mention of where in the land of Judah this newborn prince would be found. Naturally they turned to the capital city of Jerusalem and inquired at the palace of Herod. That is when they discovered another source of information, but not from King Herod. Herod summoned the chief priests and scribes and asked them to search the Scripture for a reference to where Messiah would be born. They came back and told him of the prophecy of Micah:

"But you, Bethlehem Ephrathah, though you are small among the clans of Judah, out of you will come for me one who will be ruler over Israel, whose origins are from of old, from ancient times" (Micah 5:2).

Then Herod, very troubled by the thought of some newborn king, relayed this information to the magi. They left for Bethlehem, a short distance of only seven miles. But the odd thing is this: Why did no one go with them? Wouldn't you think they would want to see if there was any substance to the story of the moving star and foreigners asking about a Jewish king? The indifference of the religious leaders to the things of God was already present long before they were to hear about a controversial man named Jesus of Nazareth.

Arriving in Bethlehem, the magi found the baby Jesus not in a stable but in a house. This suggests that they may have arrived there months after Jesus' birth. Never mind that we cannot think of the Nativity scene without thinking of the wise men kneeling in front of Jesus in the manger. The point is that they arrived and saw Jesus with Mary his mother and fell down in adoration and worship, offering gifts suitable for royalty — gold, frankincense and myrrh.

Each of the gifts was real but also symbolic of who this child was. Gold was the metal of royalty. It was the first metal known to man because it is found in nature in a pure state. It has always been a precious metal and symbolizes the things that have enduring value. Investors invest in gold today much like stocks, and it is desirable as a stable investment that does not fluctuate much with the economy. Our currency today, in fact, is valued to the degree that it remains backed by a sufficient quantity of gold. So a costly gift for a royal child would suggest a gift of gold.

I like to think that this gift of gold was God's way of providing for the expenses of Jesus' family during their journeys away from Nazareth. Being a poor man, Joseph would not have had many financial resources to pay for the trip to Bethlehem and for temporary living quarters there. Nor would he have been able to finance the trip to Egypt and living expenses there to escape the terrorist activities designed by Herod to eliminate a newborn king. Joseph and Mary were refugees, and the gift of gold was needed for their provision and safety while exiled in Egypt.

Gold reminds us that Jesus Christ was truly a king. He was not a crowned head of state but one who rightly claimed to have the kingly authority of Almighty God. He spoke of those who followed him as being in his kingdom. This gift of the wise men makes us ponder whether or not we have invited Jesus Christ to act as our king. As the familiar carol puts it, Jesus is "king forever, ceasing never, over us all to reign."

The second gift was incense. It was a fragrant spice used to purify the temple offerings and make them worthy of being accepted by God. It was also a symbol used to many peoples to signify the rising of their prayers to the gods of their religion. Jews also used incense in the same way. As the smoke rises, so does the prayer.

We bring Jesus our incense when we approach him as God, not just a great man or prophet. We cannot soften the bold and direct claims he made to be God in human form. That is why we come to him rightly and ask forgiveness for our sins, as only God can do that. That is why we are not

simply to see him as a model human being but to acknowledge him as God and give him the worship that he has every
right to receive. As the carol puts it, "Incense owns a deity
nigh. Prayer and praising, gladly raising, worship him God
most high."

Finally there was the gift of myrrh. As gold speaks of royalty and incense speaks of deity, myrrh speaks of the suffering
and death of the Savior. We sing, "Myrrh is mine, its bitter
perfume breathes a life of gathering gloom; sorrowing, sigh-
ing, bleeding, dying, sealed in the stone cold tomb."

Myrrh was used in the ancient world as an anesthetic to
deaden pain and also for embalming the dead. We cannot
know just what was in the mind of the wise men as they
chose this gift, but we do know that the Old Testament clearly
prophecies that the Messiah would be rejected and killed.
Perhaps they heard of such Scriptures. In any case we know
that Jesus himself was conscious of an eternal plan in the
mind of God that would require his death. Quite literally we
can say that Jesus was born to die.

You and I bring Jesus our gift of myrrh when we recognize
and accept him in his role of Savior of the world. He took
our death that we might have his life. Paul never could get
over the thrill of it: "The life I now live I live by faith in the
son of God who loved me and gave himself for me" (Gal.
2:20). Peter put it this way: "Christ died for sins once for all,
the righteous for the unrighteous, to bring you to God" (1
Peter 3:18). Gratitude for this pardon made at such great
cost is the kind of myrrh we can lay at the manger as we
celebrate the Savior's birth.

As I read this familiar part of the Christmas story I am
reminded that what counts with God is whether or not I
have the seeking attitude modeled by the wise men. God
had said through Jeremiah, "You will seek me and find me

when you seek me with all your heart" (Jer. 29:13). Jesus said, "Seek and you will find" (Matt. 7:7). The writer of Hebrews said, "Whoever would draw near to God must believe that he exists and that he rewards those who seek him" (Heb. 11:6). It is not what you know but what you do about what you know that makes the difference. Ironically, the people who ought to have celebrated the birth of Christ did not, and those whom you would least expect to do so did!

Coming to Christ is for many people a long and arduous journey of seeking. It takes determination and patience. The distance is not geographical but psychological, intellectual or emotional. And we must remember that the magi got to their destination late. But that did not matter. They got there. If you have trouble with doubts why put the burden of proof on your faith? Begin to doubt your doubts for a change and look honestly at the impressive evidence that Scripture is giving you fact not fiction. If you come to Christ as a teenager it is great. If you come later in life it is great. It is not when or how which counts in the end, but only that you come to Christ.

Today pilgrims to the Holy Land visit Bethlehem to see the famous Church of the Incarnation that was built over the site of Jesus' birth. The entrance door is narrow and low. Only one person can enter at a time, and only by stooping. Faith is an individual thing and requires a humble spirit. Having to bow as you enter brings this to mind. Each time I pass through that entrance I remember that faith begins with recognizing the true identity of the baby born in that place. The child was no less than God in human form, and therefore deserves our worship, not merely our respect. When I am there I feel that I am standing on holy ground. I have felt that in a lesser degree when standing on the battlefield at Gettysburg or in the room where the Declaration of Independence was signed in Philadelphia. How much more is the feeling of awe I have when standing next to the shrine marking the place where God Almighty came down from heaven and "for us and for our salvation was made man" (Apostles' Creed).

Then, once inside the church, one of the first things your guide will point out is the fact that this is the oldest Christian church in the Holy Land. That is because many other churches were destroyed during the Middle Ages in the invasion of the conquering Muslim warriors. But this church was spared. You learn why as you look up and see just below the roofline some colored frescoes showing the wise men from Persia offering their gifts to Jesus. This was the reason the invaders did not destroy the church. As they entered the sanctuary they looked up and saw people depicted on the murals who looked just like themselves! How could they destroy a building that honored the wise men from Persia, a country from which these same invaders hailed?

Wise men from Persia laying gifts in front of Jesus also symbolizes for me that Jesus is everybody's Christ. Yes, He was born a Jew. He belonged to his race, his culture, his time, but he really belongs to every generation, race, culture and nation. In a day when it is fashionable to believe that there are many ways to reach God, Jesus challenges us to see how this cannot be. All religions are not saying the same thing. Every other religion is a program of what we must do to please God. Christianity is the only religion that says that it is not a question of what we do for God but what He did for us. No one prayed that God would someday act out the story of Jesus the way it happened. Yet God in His mercy was willing to give us just what we needed most: a savior. And there are no other saviors but the one who came at Christmas. "Salvation is found in no one else, for there is no other name under heaven given to men by which we must be saved" (Acts 4:12). There is no other name because there can be no other name. Either Christianity is universally true for everybody or else it is true for nobody, not even those who happen to think it is true!

God is the author of truth, not confusion. He would not reveal Himself in one way to some people and in contradictory ways to other people. That means that those exclusive claims of Jesus to be the way, the truth and the life are not arrogant and boastful but plain statements of fact. The exclusivity of Jesus is the secret of his inclusivity. He must not and does not have any rivals. He is the full revelation of the only God there is. Jesus was simply stating a fact by saying, "No one comes to the Father except through me" (John 14:6).

The wise men remind us that there will always be misconceptions about who Jesus is. Like them, people will always be looking in the wrong places at first. But these mysterious figures from far away can be our models nonetheless. They can symbolize for us the importance of persistence in searching for Christ with an inquiring mind, of not being discouraged by obstacles, and to give him the gift of our worship as God and King.

The Innkeeper

We do not know his name, but he played more than a bit part in the story. It was the innkeeper in Bethlehem who caused the Nativity scene to look the way it does. If somehow we could ask him to step out of the Christmas story where he has no lines and ask him to remain in character we would want to ask him about that scene at the front door of his inn. We would ask, "Why did you turn Joseph and Mary away?" He would answer, "Well, obviously, because there was no room. Others had come here first and taken up the few spaces available. They were so demanding, especially those Roman soldiers. I barely had time to go to the door and see who was there. I could see that they really needed lodging, and that Mary was pregnant, but how was I to know who they were? Had I known I would have given up my own bed. But they just looked like so many other travelers here for the census registration. So, under the circumstances I gave them the best accommodations I had, the stable out back. It was at least a quiet place of shelter. It was not at all fitting, but it was the best I could do."

No, the place where animals are fed and stabled was not fitting for the birth of any baby, and especially for the birth of the Savior of the world. Mary did not have the privacy any woman would want. People were coming and going and may well have heard Mary's cries as her contractions increased. I can picture Joseph having to keep chasing away curious onlookers who came to gawk.

When the baby came they wrapped him in the traditional strips of cloth. It was a square piece with a long strip from one of the corners and was used as a diaper. The attached strip was used to hold the diaper and cover the body. The feeding bin known as the manger served as the only available crib.

Personally, I think that history has been less than sympathetic with the innkeeper. And when you think about the man Jesus grew up to be, the teaching about humility that was always on his lips, I don't think God minded one bit that Jesus was born in a stable. The circumstances are actually fitting for someone who would later have no residence he could call his own, "no place to lay my head," as he told a wannabe follower who did not know what it would mean to be a disciple (Luke 9:57,58).

I wonder how many sermons have been preached on that line in Luke's Christmas story about this unknown man we call the innkeeper. "There was no room for them in the inn" (Luke 1:7). For that scenario is more than just a fact in the narrative. It is a timeless parable. Like that inn so is the condition of many a human heart and mind — preoccupied and busy with meeting the urgent demands of prior commitments.

This is why for too many people Christmas is a holiday they do not enjoy. They get so wrapped up in the social and commercial aspects of buying, decorating, partying, cooking, traveling, mailing, buying a tree, wrapping presents, etc. they miss the meaning behind it all. It becomes only a tradition whose original meaning has been forgotten.

There is nothing wrong with partying and feasting except when those doing it have forgotten why there should be a party or a feast. Many have done so. There is nothing wrong with exchanging gifts when it serves as a reminder that Christmas is all about the gift that God sent to the world in the person of Jesus. There is nothing wrong with buying a tree and setting it up inside the living room with decorations. Being an evergreen it is a perfect symbol of life that has no ending, which is the gift of God to all who call Jesus Lord and Savior. There is nothing wrong with decorating the outside of the house with lighting displays, or putting colored lights all over the Christmas tree. That reminds us that Jesus said that he was the light of the world, and that when we follow him we have the light of the Holy Spirit to guide us always.

No, there is nothing wrong with calling Christmas a holiday, as it should well be set aside as a day when people are not at work and are at home with the families celebrating. After all, the word *holiday* derives from the words "holy day," a time for remembering that which is holy.

The problem of the innkeeper is with us all. We must be on guard lest our celebrating of Christmas, ironically, become the very thing that keeps us from its real meaning! The innkeeper said no to Joseph and Mary because there was literally no available space. But how much "space" have we allotted Christ in our lives? How much time are we willing to set aside to worship, to hear and read God's word, and to pray? Our interests are drawn off into so many directions, until there is no room in our lives except perhaps in the "stable" of leftover time and energy.

Why? The reason for us is the same as it was for the innkeeper. We don't know who Jesus is. If we did, we would open the front door of our hearts and minds and ask him to make himself at home. This is exactly what he said he wants to do. Listen to Jesus: "If anyone loves me, he will obey my teaching. My Father will love him, and we will come to him and make our home with him" (John 14:23).

But look at another message in this text. In Luke 2:7 we read, "because there was no room for them in the inn." It is still true today. We must not think that the world will be delighted that we have become followers of Jesus. The world today shuts him out just as it did then. There will be those who make fun of people who are so old fashioned as to believe, as Christ did, in absolute truth that is given by God, not invented by men. There are those who wish that we would blend into our culture rather than confront it. The reason we are given is the need to be more tolerant in a country growing more and more diverse.

Professor Daniel Taylor of Bethel College claims that tolerance is a new gospel in America. He points out that there are some important notions imbedded in the concept. "One is not tolerant of something unless one objects to it. I do not tolerate something I either accept or am indifferent to because it requires nothing of me. If tolerance requires an initial objection then conservatives, ironically, may be much more tolerant than liberals because there are so many more things to which they object. The least tolerant person is the person who accepts everything because such a person is not required to overcome any internal objections.... Is Chesterton on to something when he says tolerance is the virtue of those who don't believe in anything? Too much of what passes as tolerance in America is not the result of principled judgment but is simple moral indifference." [16]

Was Jesus being intolerant by his claims to be the only way to God? I think not. Our task will be to help others see that no one really wants a God who has competitors. Moreover, a God with competitors is by definition not God! If anything is clear from the Bible it is that there is only one God. "Hear O Israel: The Lord our God, the Lord is one" (Deut. 6:4). "Turn to me and be saved, all you ends of the earth; for I am God and there is no other" (Isaiah 45:22). This is the God whose visit to our planet and our human race has shown us who He is. There are no other choices because there can be none.

The good news for us is that even though so many people do not have room for the God who came to us at Christmas has plenty of room for anyone and everyone. "If I be lifted up (on the cross) I will draw all men unto myself" (John 12:32). "God so loved the world (a very inclusive phrase) that He gave His only Son...." (John 3:16). "Trust in God, trust also in me. In my father's house are many rooms, ("resting places," as the Greek literally means). I am going there to prepare a place for you. And if I go and prepare a place for you I will come again and take you to be with me that you also may be where I am" (John 14:6). There is nothing narrow minded about a God who extends an invitation to anyone and everyone who will listen and accept it. The challenge is for all of us to see that Jesus Christ is the Savior of the whole world, of every nation, race, and generation of people. He chooses them; He then waits for an answer to His RSVP. Have you ever given Him yours?

Simeon and Anna

Luke gives us a brief portrait of two all-but-forgotten people in the Christmas story, Simeon and Anna. Let's find out what it was that motivated Luke to include them in his account (Luke 2:25-35). The background is the time just after Jesus was born (eight days later) when Joseph and Mary had brought their baby to the temple in Jerusalem for dedication and for circumcision. The fact that this was important to them tells us about the kind of home in which Jesus was to be raised. It was a home where from the beginning of his life Jesus would be informed about and submitted to the commandments of God.

The Jewish law said that the firstborn male child was to be consecrated to the Lord. Many did not honor that requirement but Joseph and Mary took it seriously, as we might expect. While Joseph and Mary were there in the temple that day they met a special person by the name of Simeon. Little is known about him except what Luke tells us. We are not told his age, though traditionally we have thought of him as elderly.

Two words describe Simeon's character: righteous and devout. A righteous person is one who is dedicated to the keeping of God's laws. He defined right and wrong by the word of God. Without that benchmark for defining the boundaries of life's playing field, you have no way of telling fair from foul, truth from error, good from bad. A righteous person — that is, one who is just and fair — wants to know and keep the boundaries. Simeon was also devout. He desired to please God in word and deed and to take Him seriously. We are also told that Simeon was "waiting for the consolation of Israel." This is another way of saying that he was looking for the Messiah to come. Here was a man who got up every morning and wondered, "Maybe today I will see the Messiah." And every day he had gone home disappointed but not discouraged. He trusted God's promise, and kept the faith over a long period of time.

The context suggests that this was not some temporary manifestation of the Holy Spirit but an abiding presence in his life. In addition we are told that Simeon had a private revelation of the Spirit that he would not die before he had a chance to see the Messiah with his own eyes.

Then one day it happened. Joseph and Mary and Jesus came through those temple doors and the Spirit of God prompted Simeon to know that this child was, in fact, the long-awaited Messiah. He burst out in a song of praise to God, a hymn that is one of the earliest of Christian hymns, known by its Latin name, *Nunc Dimittis*. It is a song for the joyful ending of a life that has known the peace of God. One interesting detail is Simeon's choice of a Greek word for the opening of the song. He began by referring to God as his *despota*. This is the word from which our word despot is derived. A despot is one who has absolute authority over others. It has a negative connotation to us in English and generally refers to one who rules as a tyrant. That meaning, however, was not in Simeon's mind. He was saying something positive and commendable. God was for him the master who had sovereign authority over him and deserved his total allegiance and submission as a servant. He was glad to accept that role.

After singing his song, he spoke a prophecy to Joseph and Mary. He blessed them and said to Mary, "This child is appointed for the falling and rise of many in Israel" (Luke 2:34). What did he mean by that?

In the Old Testament it was prophesied that the Messiah would be like a stone which some people would trip and stumble over, but which others would find to be a stepping stone to more life. The idea is that with Christ there can be no permanent neutrality. We are either for him or against him. Depending on our response to him we stand under God's judgment or God's blessing. If we go our own way and reject Christ, his gospel will not be good news but bad news. It will mean that God will allow us to have the consequences of our choice, and that will mean separation from him. But if we accept Christ and his claims and believe that it is for our sins that he died on the cross, he will then be our Savior. To use Simeon's words, it will be for our "rising" and not our "falling."

Then Simeon went on to say that some people would oppose Jesus when he grows up. Jesus would become "a sign that is spoken against" (vs. 34). The word for sign is a strong one, and is often used in the New Testament for a miracle. In his ministry Jesus did many such signs that were intended to communicate who he was. But, as the record shows, some people found reason to believe that Jesus was doing these signs by the power of Satan, not God. How that must have hurt Jesus.

Then the prophecy became more personal and foreboding. As he turned to Mary and looked her straight in the eye, he said with a tone of sadness in his voice, "and a sword will pierce your own soul too" (Luke 2:35). This can only refer to the cross where Jesus was put to death. Think of Mary standing there watching while the Roman centurion thrust a spear into Jesus' body. She must have felt that a sword had been thrust into her soul as well.

I can imagine that Mary never forgot that meeting with Simeon when Jesus was dedicated. How could she? Later, when she was elderly and telling Luke everything about the way the story of Jesus all began, she remembered how Simeon's prophecies had all come true.

Now Luke tells us about Anna, an elderly woman who, like Simeon, was focused on waiting for God to send the long-awaited Messiah. (See Luke 2:36-38.) Like Simeon, she waited every day, each day eagerly anticipating the possibility that this day might be the one. She had been a widow for a long time, and had enjoyed only seven years of marriage. Now she was eighty-four. Her life had been given over to a ministry of prayer and fasting there in the temple. She is defined here as a "prophetess," that is, a woman gifted to speak the word of God in a special and personal message.

For me, Anna is the one who models how God can alleviate the pain of loneliness. Most of her life she was alone. But she did not let her disappointment or sorrow lead to bitterness. Instead she was gracious and godly. She kept God at the center of her life, not at the margins. As she grew older her faith grew even stronger.

It is interesting that Luke should tell us that a life of service to God might be one of fasting and praying. Usually we think that the people God calls to full-time service are the professionals. These are the ordained clergy, missionaries,

Bible teachers, and chaplains in the armed services, prisons and hospitals. But here we learn that there are many other kinds of ministries. Anna was called to a lay ministry of worship and prayer. God had been preparing her for the unique privilege of seeing and recognizing the original Christmas gift of the Savior. "Coming up to them that very moment she gave thanks to God, and spoke about the child to all who were looking forward to the redemption of Jerusalem" (vs. 38).

There we see two distinct earmarks of a genuine believer. Anna regarded her privilege of seeing the Savior as an occasion to say thank you to God. Gratitude is a primary virtue of those who know who Jesus is. Also, Anna realized that to know the Savior is to accept the responsibility for telling others that the Savior had come and that his name was Jesus.

What can we learn about these two almost forgotten people of Christmas? We learn that God is a promise-keeping God. He promised He would come — and He did! Simeon and Anna knew that and lived in light of it. Every morning they got up and said to themselves, "This might be the day." One morning they were both right.

You and I are also to be waiting for the coming of the Messiah, Jesus. Not as Simeon and Anna did, for his first coming, but for his **second** coming. That promise is just as sure as the promise Simeon and Anna held on to as they eagerly anticipated the birth of Jesus. But we live in a time when 2,000 years have passed and Jesus has not yet returned. We are inclined to think that this means that the second coming of Christ has been postponed indefinitely.

The apostle Peter wrote a letter to people with similar doubts about the return of the Messiah. He called them "scoffers." "They will say, 'Where is this "coming" he promised? Ever since our fathers died, everything goes on as it has since the beginning of creation.' But do not forget this one thing, dear friends: With the Lord a day is like a thousand years and a thousand years is like a day. The Lord is not slow in keeping his promise, as some understand slowness. He is patient with you, not wanting anyone to perish, but everyone to come to repentance" (2 Peter 3:4,8,9).

It is not a matter of whether or not Christ will return but of whether or not you and I are going to be prepared. What will motivate us to live in a state of spiritual preparedness for Jesus' return? One will be the fact that tomorrow might be that day. Jesus himself said that no one knows the day or hour and therefore everyone ought to be ready. A restaurant keeps its kitchen up to city standards of cleanliness never knowing when the health inspector will make a surprise inspection. No warnings are ever given.

Spiritually it works the same way. You do not prepare for a crisis after the crisis comes. The apostle John wrote: "And now, children, continue in him so that when he appears we may be confident and unashamed before him at his coming" (1 John 2:28). Again we find that there is no middle ground of neutrality with Christ. We will be prepared or unprepared for his return. If we have been faithful we will be confident and full of hope. If we have not been faithful we will experience only regret and shame.

The Christian, of course, has to live in the world. But we do not have to become too comfortable with the world's values. Being a Christian, however, is something like being a boat out on the water. The boat is not for staying on dry dock on the land. It is made for being in the water. But the boat is in the water; the water is NOT in the boat.

How then shall we live? Peter wrote, "You ought to live holy and godly lives as you look forward to the day of God and speed its coming.... Make every effort to be found spotless, blameless and at peace with him. Bear in mind that the Lord's patience means salvation..." (2 Peter 3: 8,11,14).

Christmas reminds us that Jesus was born as God promised. God always keeps His promises. He came to Bethlehem. And He will come again. We need to live daily in light of that coming, and be prepared whether or not it happens in our lifetime

Have you ever noticed how children behave better as Christmas approaches? They are eagerly anticipating all those presents under the Christmas tree and they dream of the joy of opening them one by one. And when they get a little rowdy and uncooperative what do Mom and Dad do? They remind them that Santa is coming and he will reward only good behavior.

You and I have a much better reason to "behave" and live godly lives. Not to make sure we get presents under the tree. Rather, to be among that group of people who will welcome Jesus at his second coming and be ready for him to judge us as truly belonging to him. We don't need to be checking off events in world history on a chart so we can know precisely when his coming is getting close, and then start to reform our lives. We just need to live for Christ day by day. It is like the ancient prayer. "Three things of thee, O Lord I pray ... to love thee more dearly, see thee more clearly, follow thee more nearly, day by day."

In the recent movie *Titanic* there was a powerful message in the scene where all the people who had not managed to get into a lifeboat now realized that death was near. Some just decided to pretend nothing was happening. They poured another drink, listened to the instrumentalists playing as they always did. They were in complete denial. But there were others who gathered to hear someone read from the New Testament book of Revelation. In that book we have the promise that Jesus Christ has conquered death and promises all his followers a heavenly home. These people were singing "Nearer my God to thee." They were prepared for heaven.

Likewise some people live as though Christ had not come at Christmas and as though he were not going to come back and call his own to heaven. But he will. We are not to wonder about when, but simply to be living day by day in a state of spiritual readiness, as though today might be that day. Simeon and Anna woke each morning with such joyful anticipation. We should do the same.

Chapter Seven

God Is Not Santa Claus

Many people assume that God operates on a system of rewards and punishments. How many times in the Christmas season we hear the song, "You better watch out, you better not cry, you better not pout, I'm telling you why — Santa Claus is coming to town.... He knows when you are sleeping; he knows when you're awake. He knows if you've been bad or good so be good for goodness' sake...."

Most of us grow up thinking that if we are good we will be rewarded, and if we are bad we will be punished. We have become used to this system and actually believe that there is nothing wrong with it. After all, it seems to work. People are motivated that way.

The problem comes when we abuse the system, and relate to other people on a basis of having to earn or deserve their approval. This cripples us emotionally by leading us to conclude that our self-worth is built on and sustained by the approval of other people. And yet how often, after a sincere effort at winning someone else's favor, some unappreciative comment destroys the self-assurance we have worked so hard to attain.

So many have tried to earn the approval of other significant people in their lives but never received it. Parents were never satisfied with good grades; only A's were acceptable. Then there was the boss who was always finding fault with his employees and never gave his approval. Perhaps it was a coach or maybe a music or art instructor in middle school who could have made such a difference if just some word of encouragement and affirmation had been shown, but the students never received it. As we grow up there is one thing we fear most of all — not measuring up in the eyes of parents, teachers, and peers. It is the gnawing feeling of guilt from not being accepted and approved by the significant people in our lives.

In our society there is a strong tendency to think the same way about God — that life is all about behaving in order to win God's approval. We are likely to think that we are to do right because God, like Santa, has a list and He is checking it twice. He knows who's naughty and who's nice. Our goal, then, conscious or not, becomes that of making sure that we have been nice more times than we have been naughty. We obey simply out of a desire for rewards or out of a fear of punishment.

I recall vividly the day when a former member of one of the congregations I served came to me and asked for some counseling about a personal problem. He got right to the point. He said, "I can't get out of my mind something that I did years ago. I am not going to say what it was but it was so bad that if I were God, I would not forgive me."

I did not need to know what he had done. What concerned me was learning that he had been living with a Santa Claus theology for many years. He went through the motions of worship, and heard me, his pastor, pronounce the absolution after the general confession but it never seemed to relieve his conscience. The reason was he never felt that he qualified for God's forgiveness. I said, "Let's look at a Bible passage together. Turn to Ephesians 2:8, 9." We read it. "For by grace you have been saved through faith, and this is not your own doing; it is the gift of God not of works, lest anyone should boast."

Without using the phrase, I went on to show him that Santa Claus theology is based on pride, as Paul clearly said. Suppose you could win God's favor by doing good deeds. Who would determine the standard of what is good? What grade would be passing? Would God grade on a bell-shaped curve? Does He compare us with others? Whom? St. Francis? Mother Teresa? If He did, we would unconsciously be asking Him to approve of some degree of self-centeredness. So unless we can be perfect the whole system is flawed.

Instead, Paul says that being saved, being put in a right relationship with God, comes by grace as an unearned and undeserved gift from God. It is not our own doing. How hard that is for us to accept. We want to take some credit for being good and doing good. Why bother if it does not get us something we would otherwise not have?

But consider what a rescue operation is like. Let us imagine you are caught in a storm when you are out on a lake in a small boat. The boat capsizes and you struggle to stay afloat. Fortunately, a rescue boat crew spots you and speeds to where you are. Would you prefer that the boat back off a hundred yards or so in order that you might swim over to it and receive only part of a rescue? No, you would want to tread water until the boat came alongside and tossed you a life preserver. You would simply let the rescue boat do all the rescuing.

The rescue operation of God is not half grace and half human effort. It is all grace. Grace is what enabled St. Paul to deal with his own painful memories. Talk about painful memories! Which of us can match Paul's haunting past? He had done his level best to stamp out the Christian faith! He stood watching while Stephen died by stoning for his faith in the risen Christ. But later Paul had a dramatic encounter with that same risen Christ who changed him from being an enemy of Christ to being the chief apostle. Salvation is not by good deeds counterbalancing bad deeds. It is by grace, through faith, as God uses a divine eraser to forgive our sins by the payment made for them by his own Son's death on the cross.

This is the point I wanted my friend to see. I turned to First John and asked him to read out loud verses 9 and 10. Here are the apostle's words: "If we confess our sins he is faithful and just and will forgive us our sins and purify us from all unrighteousness." I asked, "Did you notice that word *all*"? He said he did. I said, "Then if what is so hurtful for you to remember is not included in 'all unrighteousness,' you are saying that John is mistaken." He saw the logic of it. We concluded that Jesus did die for any and all sin, and that there is no wrongdoing not covered by his atoning sacrifice on the cross. I am happy to say that sometime later, after some concentrated prayer and subsequent visits, God was able to heal his memories and give him the assurance of salvation he never had.

One problem with Santa Claus theology is that no one can truly be good enough. When an expert in the Scriptures came to Jesus and asked what he would have to do to gain eternal life. Jesus asked him what was written in the law of God. The man answered by quoting the commandment to love God completely with heart, soul, mind and strength, and the neighbor as oneself. Jesus said, "Right. Do this and you will live." (Luke 10:25) Jesus knew, of course, that this was the goal we strive for but never can reach. Some are better than others at it, but no one is able to be good enough.

What we must avoid is any suggestion that Christianity is something naughty people need and nice people don't. It is not that God does not appreciate niceness in people. He truly does. But He knows that self-improvement is not enough. In fact those who do it often become more difficult for God to reach. C.S. Lewis writes, "We must not suppose that, even if we succeeded in making everyone nice, we should have saved their souls. A world of nice people, content in their niceness, looking no further, turned away from God, would be just as desperately in need of salvation as a miserable world, and might even be more difficult to save." [17]

It is like the situation of two teenagers who pass the movie theater and decide to see a film. They open their wallets. One has two dollars and the other has three. The price of admission is six dollars. One misses it by three dollars, the other by four. Neither can get in. It is the same spiritually. Some people are much nicer and less naughty than others but they are still not good enough and never will be good enough. That is why everyone needs the Savior.

Another problem with Santa Claus theology is that we are apt to think that we, by trying harder to be nice, might so please God that He would take us out of the category of sinners. Jesus told a story about a tax collector and a Pharisee (Luke 18:9-14). The Pharisee congratulated himself on his good deeds, his discipline of fasting and giving, his record of moral purity and honesty. His pride was blinding him into thinking that he no longer needed to ask for God's forgiveness. He was trusting instead in his own goodness. On the other hand, the tax collector, in honest confession, admitted that he really did need God's forgiveness. Jesus said that only the tax collector's prayer was heard.

St. Nick and St. Paul cannot both be correct. If Paul is wrong, if being made right with God is partly or wholly our own doing, if it is not a gift but a prize for good behavior, then the gospel message is totally irrelevant. What is worse, the rescue operation of Christ was for nothing. It was a tragic mistake and Jesus died needlessly. But Paul is right. A right relationship with God is a purely undeserved gift of love.

Whenever I am tempted to think that being nice and not naughty should give me some credit with God I am re-minded that **the only real contribution I can make to my salvation is the sin from which I want to be saved!** Yes, it really is all God's doing. Not mostly, but **all.**

Here is how Peter put it: "Christ died for sins, once for all, the righteous for the unrighteous to bring you to God" (I Peter 3:18). Christ paid our sin debt in full. But He will not force us to accept that payment. He waits for us to see the need for it and ask for it.

Someone will ask, "Then why bother trying to be good? If it is all grace then I will be forgiven anyway and I need not make the effort any longer." Paul heard that argument in his day. "What shall we say, then? Shall we go on sinning so that grace may increase? By no means. We died to sin; how can we live in it any longer?" (Romans 6:1,2). Paul was saying that grace is not a license to sin. God's forgiveness must not be abused or taken for granted. Rather, if we are sincere in our asking for God's grace we will actually want to say thank you and please God by a determination to do right. We have a new motivation for being nice and doing good. It is not to earn or deserve the favor of God, but rather to say thank you in appreciation for the gift we did not deserve.

I like the way the great Protestant reformer Martin Luther put it. He said, "Good works do not make a man good but a good man will do good works." [18] By that he meant that it is God's unearned forgiveness that makes us good in His sight, not our good deeds. Then, after we have been made right with God, our gratitude for that becomes our motivation for doing good works. We do good not to get God's favor, but because we are grateful to Him for giving it to us through Christ's death on the cross.

How about you? Is your striving to be a good person motivated by your wanting God to take note on His list and mark you down as deserving of a reward for your behavior? Or, on the other hand, do you see that the real God is one whose approval you already have? He is the God whose love for you is so real and deep that He does whatever it takes to provide you a full and free pardon for your sins.

I trust that you will see by now that Santa Claus theology is plain wrong. What keeps us from being naughty and trying instead to be nice is not the thought of reward or punishment. No, it is a motivation so much purer and unselfish — the motivation of wanting to say thank you for what God did for us on the cross. We want only to be able to go on through life reconciled to Him and to find at the end of our lives a warm welcome at the gate of heaven.

Chapter Eight

The Difference
Christmas Makes

To ponder the question, "Did the coming of Jesus make any difference?" is like asking a man who has just been rescued from drowning, "Did our coming to your rescue make any difference?" He would say, "You saved my life!" But even that comparison falls short of the kind of saving that Jesus the Savior does for us the lifeguard prevents the swimmer from physical death. But the Savior of the world prevents the sinner from spiritual death and offers instead a life that literally lasts forever. Surely that is what Paul had in mind when he described the coming of Christ into the world as God's "indescribable gift" (2 Cor. 9:15).

When we ask about the difference Christmas makes we can answer in the following ways:

♦ Because Jesus came we no longer need to wonder about the nature and character of God. The story of Christmas is that **Jesus is like God and God is like Jesus.**

There is something in all of us human beings that is akin to the "show me" mentality of people from Missouri. If we cannot have proof that something we hear is believable, we are apt to want compelling evidence that it is true. In this regard, the disciple Philip was so much like us. He was not being skeptical, but rather wanting a stronger faith when he came to Jesus and said, "Lord show us the Father and we shall be satisfied." Jesus replied, "How can you say, 'Show us the Father?' Have I been with you so long Philip and you do not know me? If you have seen me you have seen the Father" (John 14:9).

That is a startling claim, isn't it? And yet, it is true. We cannot know, of course, what a camera lens would have seen and what the developed picture would show us of Jesus. Much as we might wish for a snapshot of Jesus it is just as well that we do not have one. This way we are not likely to focus on the physical characteristics of Jesus. When he said, "If you have seen me you have seen the Father," he was not being literal. God the Father does not have a body that resembles the body of Jesus.

No, what Jesus meant was that his thoughts, words and deeds were clues as to the nature of the one, eternal and invisible God. In Jesus, God has an intelligible and human focus. We see His character in terms we can understand. As someone has said, "Jesus is the human face of God." As John's gospel puts it, "No one has ever seen God; the only Son, who is in the bosom of the Father, has made him known" (John 1:18). "He is the image of the invisible God" (Col. 1:15). He is the "stamp of God's nature" (Hebrews 1:3). The image refers to the impression stamped on a coin to convey an exact likeness. We think of God as we see Him in the words and deeds and personality of Jesus.

"The Word became flesh and dwelt among us" (John 1:14). The actual Greek says, "pitched his tent." The idea is that of a temporary dwelling. The Jewish people know that they trace their ancestry way back to a time when as a people they were nomadic tribes camping out in tents. Abraham, in fact, was called a "wandering Aramean" (Deut 26:5). He was the father of a nation always on the move to a promised land. John gives us a powerful image as he likens God's coming into the world to a person setting up tent for a temporary stay. Yet this is precisely what it was. "God with us" is a brief but accurate way of speaking about the fact that God is for us and always concerned about our welfare.

It suggests that God is for us in that He takes our side. It means that God cares for us enough to want to send the Savior, knowing full well it would mean the cross. The corollary truth to that is, as Paul says, "If God is for us who can be against us? He who spared not his own son but gave him up for us all, how shall he not with him freely give us all things?" (Romans 8: 32). The logic is that if God cared enough to come into the world to suffer and die on the cross for our sins, it stands to reason that He is truly and totally committed to our well being now.

♦ Christmas matters because it shows us a God who takes the initiative and does all He can to help us to know Him. He is truly approachable. He is not remote and aloof, running the universe and unconcerned about our human situation. He does not want us simply to know about Him but to know Him in a personal relationship of trust and belief. Listen to the apostle John: "This is how God showed his love among us: He sent his one and only Son into the world that we might live through him. This is love: not that we loved God but that he loved us and sent his son as an atoning sacrifice for our sins" (1 John 4: 9,10).

I cannot overemphasize this distinction between a religion that is designed to get the attention of God and ultimately His favor, and true religion that works just the other way around. Christianity is a religion in which God acts first, and then human beings react and respond to God's prior action. What this means is that genuine faith is not a strategy but a response. "We love because He first loved us" (1 John 4:19). It is a response in which you and I discover that the God we want to know has already done everything He could possibly do on our behalf. The "old, old story of Jesus and his love" is the story which, when we hear it, calls for us to answer the invitation to say yes or no. Either we accept our need for the Savior God sent or we say by our disinterest that we think we have no need of a Savior at all.

◆ Christmas matters because it is proof that God cares about us enough to walk in our skin, so to speak, and to experience everything it means to be one of His own creatures. In Christ, God knows what it means to be tempted as we are. He knows how it feels to lose a dear friend, as was the case in the death of his friend Lazarus. He knows what it means to be betrayed by someone close to him. He knows what it means to be disappointed when people decided they would not follow him any longer, or when they obviously missed the main point of his teaching about humility and service.

What this means for us is that we do not have to explain to God what we are going through. You name it and Jesus has already been through it first hand. He knows and understands our situation.

During my training for the ordained ministry I spent a summer working in a large hospital in Minneapolis. I was trained in how to make helpful hospital visits and bring comfort to people facing various treatments and operations. I will never forget the time when I was introduced to a small group of people known as the "Colostomy Club." This was a volunteer group of men and women who gave of their time to speak to patients who needed this operation. The club members were most effective because they had all gone through the operation successfully and were leading normal lives. How much more convincing was a word of encouragement from a fellow patient. Members of that team could give not just empathy but genuine sympathy gained from a shared experience.

When you are facing pain, loneliness, rejection, disappointment, misunderstanding, grief, take comfort in the fact that Jesus has been where you are. He knows and understands. He can and does give you sympathy of having been through whatever you are facing and much, much more. Here is how the author of the letter to the Hebrews puts it: "For we do not have a high priest who is unable to sympathize with our weaknesses, but we have one who has been tempted in every way, just as we are, yet without sin" (Hebrews 4:15).

♦ When I contemplate the Christmas card scene of the birth of Jesus I am reminded that circumstances of my life do not really matter so much as I thought. I marvel that this baby, of all babies, should have such a humble birth in a stable. Not surprisingly this is the child who grew into the man who taught that happiness has nothing to do with possessions or position or achievement or recognition. Paul put it this way: "You know the grace of our Lord Jesus Christ, that though he was rich, yet for your sake he became poor, so that by his poverty you might become rich" (2 Cor. 8:9).

That is literally true. Just think of what it would be like to live in some primitive part of the world where indoor plumbing, good schools, adequate medical care, computers, phones, cars and such are unknown. It would be quite an adjustment for anyone moving there from most anywhere in America. But consider what poverty Jesus chose in coming to this world. Do you think Bill Gates is rich? By comparison Jesus was so much richer that Bill Gates looks as poor as a beggar. Jesus left the glory of heaven where every angel was at his beck and call. He was more creative than a thousand Michelangelos. But he did not consider equality with God something to be "grasped" but instead he laid his divine glory and prerogatives aside. He was born into a good and godly family, but a family that was materially poor.

Yet so many people today are likely to feel that the good life means that they must have the best car, the best house, and the best position. People do "grasp" and cling to this and feel that it makes for happiness. Christmas tells us that this is a lie. Poverty and riches need to be redefined. The really poor people are not poor in things but poor in the things of God. They are indulging the self. The truly rich people do not need worldly wealth but are putting self behind and in humility finding the satisfaction that comes from lightening the burdens of others.

♦   It reminds me that the ways of God are so different from the ways of the world. Caesar Augustus issued a decree that the whole Roman Empire must have a census for purposes of taxation. It meant that all would have to go to their hometown to register. No exceptions and no excuses. No one could disobey the command of Caesar.

But God's decree is more like an invitation than a command. God invites some shepherds to follow some clues about a baby lying in a feeding bin, a manger. They decide to go and check it out and they find it is just as the angel said. This was to be the method Jesus would use in making disciples. When he approached a potential follower, he simply invited them to go with him. They were given a choice. It would not be an easy choice. No one would be required to follow. He always respected our freedom of choice. It is the same in our day. The issue is what we will do or not do with that invitation.

♦   It matters because Christmas shows me that I do not have to comprehend what God does in order to benefit from it. For example, I do not know how the computer on which I am typing these words can store them and print them out, but that is no reason for me to go back to my old typewriter or to pen and paper. I like the verse in the Christmas hymn: "I know not how that Bethlehem's babe could in the godhead be; I only know that the manger child has brought God's love to me." Christmas should always be a mystery because it is no less than a miracle. We should not even try to understand it because it is more than our human minds can possibly grasp.

♦ Christmas matters because it tells me that God cares about what happens in our world of time, space and history. Time and eternity intersected at Christmas! This is why we date our calendars from birth of Christ. I remember, as perhaps you do, seeing the first photograph of the earth taken from outer space, looking back from the spacecraft. The astronauts described the experience of seeing it outside their capsule window, as if they could reach out and hold it in their hands. To them the earth looked like just another planet. But each of them knew that this marble ball floating in the blackness of outer space contained everything and everyone they had known and loved. Christmas tells us that God is not a divine creator who made the universe, wound it up like a clock and then let it run by itself. Nor does He regard this planet as just one of many in various solar systems He created. He regards this planet earth as the home of human beings, His special creation. "The earth is the Lord's and everything in it; the world and all who live in it" (Ps. 24:1).

More than a century ago the philosophy building at Harvard University had engraved above the doorway the famous saying of the Greek philosopher Epictetus: "Man is the measure of all things." But at the turn of the century that inscription was removed and a new one taken from Scripture put in its place: "What is man that thou art mindful of him?" It was the question asked by the psalmist in Psalm 8, a question that contains an assumption, namely that God knows and cares about our well-being. Harvard may well have become more secular since those days, but that inscription over the steps is a constant reminder to modern students that God has taken the initiative in making himself known to those who seek Him. God is truly mindful of His human creatures.

J. B. Phillips wrote a story to illustrate this truth. He used several angel figures to make his point. It seems that a senior angel is showing a junior angel around the universe. They look at whirling galaxies and blazing stars, and then fly across great expanses of space until they reach one galaxy of billions of stars.

The senior angel points to a small sphere turning slowly on its axis and looking very inconsequential, something like a dirty tennis ball. He says to the younger angel, "I want you to watch that one particularly."

"Why, what is so special about that one?" he asked.

"That planet and only that planet is the renowned Visited Planet."

"Do you mean to tell me," he asked, "that our great and glorious Prince went down in person to that fifth-rate little ball? That He stooped so low as to become one of those creeping, crawling creatures on that floating ball?"

"I do," the senior angel said, "and I don't think He would like you to call them 'creeping, crawling creatures' in that tone of voice. He loves them, strange as it may seem to us, and went down to visit them to lift them up to be like him."

The younger angel looked blank. Such a thought was beyond his comprehension.[19]

And it is beyond ours. But it is just as true...wonderfully true!

Chapter Nine

The Other Nativity

The irony about Christmas is the fact that we can think we are celebrating it when we really aren't! We can easily make Christmas into a kind of fantasy or fable, and treat it as no more than a beautiful legend. Christmas is then merely a welcome escape from the hard realities of the workaday world.

The other danger is that we will secularize Christmas into an occasion for giving gifts for their own sake. Eating, partying, spending, decorating can easily become disconnected from the real reason for the season. The sad result is pure self-indulgence and pleasure seeking.

In a larger sense things now are not all that different from the first Christmas in Bethlehem. The Christmas that happened was not the Christmas that people expected. There was not even a small group of people who expected the Messiah to be born that way. People expected some mighty warrior to come, some political figure to emerge on the scene that would show Messianic credentials by finding a way to end the occupation of the Roman armies and bring glory days back to Israel.

The problem is with us today. To the degree that we want a Savior different from the one God sent we cannot meaningfully celebrate the birth of Jesus. That was the problem all through Jesus' three-year ministry. He did not conform to their expectations, and therefore they could not and did not recognize him for who he was. John's gospel says, "He was in the world and though the world was made through him, the world did not recognize him" (John 1:10). The truth is you can recognize only the person whom you have seen before.

Recently I was in a cafeteria when a friend behind me saw me and called out my name. I turned around and saw no one I recognized. Then I heard the voice again. This time I looked intently at a man waving at me. I then recognized his wife. The two are friends that I had not seen in a long time, and the man had previously worn a beard. He just did not appear to be the person I had seen before. Had I seen and spoken to him recently there would have been no problem.

It was the same at the coming of the Messiah. From his birth to his death Jesus never conformed to the image of Messiah that had become the authentic popular version. Jesus came to be a different kind of Savior. He came not to deal with all the world's problems, or even the problems of God's people, but rather the root problem behind all human problems, the problem of selfishness and sin. Until we see that Jesus is the savior sent from heaven to save us from our sins and restore us to fellowship with God, we will not find much to rejoice about in the message of the Christmas angels. We can only recognize or "know again" that which we expect to see.

But John's gospel goes on to say that there were then, as there are now, a small number of people, relatively speaking, who do recognize Christ and receive the original Christmas gift. "He came to that which was his own, but his own did not receive him. Yet to all who received him, to those who believed in his name he gave the right to become children of God — children born not of natural descent, nor of human decision or a husband's will, but born of God" (John 1:12,13). To celebrate Christmas is to receive Christ and believe in his name. That means taking Christ at face value and accepting his claims of divine authority. It means regarding him as in a class by himself, without peers or successors, a unique human being who also has a divine nature. And when we do receive and believe in this way God gives us a new status as His children. Receiving plus believing equals belonging. That is the formula for the other nativity, the new and second birth of Christ in our hearts.

You will ask, "But aren't all people God's children?" Generically they are, in that He is the creator of all mankind. Yet there is a special family relationship reserved by God for those who receive and believe in His Son Jesus. It leads to membership in a new family of which Jesus Christ is head and all baptized believers are the members. This means that a Christian is someone who has both a natural birth and a spiritual birth, a natural family and a spiritual family. This extended family is called the Christian Church in any and all of its denominational branches.

The apostle John discounts wrong notions about this second nativity. Look at the disclaimers. First, he says that Christians are not born of natural descent or blood. For example, as a son I realize that my parents gave me an introduction to Christian faith but I did not become a Christian because they were already believers. Faith is not inherited. If children of believing parents automatically became believers without wanting or choosing to do so they would not qualify as believers at all! We choose to believe.

When Jesus invited people to follow him, he respected their right to say no. In fact on one occasion he discouraged some would-be followers who had not thought through what they were getting into (Luke 9:57ff). Nor did Jesus go to religious people and assume that they would make the best disciples. By inviting fishermen and tax collectors he showed that there is absolutely nothing about being a Christian that is predetermined by the faith or non-faith of our parents or grandparents. First generation Christians are the only kind there are.

Secondly, John says that human decision or human effort is not involved in this second birth. As Americans we are used to thinking that we can accomplish anything we decide to do. We dream impossible dreams and then make them come true: "Progress is our most important product," the old G.E. commercial said. Think of the products available to us in 1901 and the products available in 2001! Think of all the challenges to "try harder" which have resulted in marvelous accomplishments. But this is not the same in the spiritual realm. You do not become a Christian by will power and sheer determination. No, Santa Claus theology, as we have seen, is a wrong notion. In the spiritual realm the action is all on God's part. "By grace you have been saved through faith", Paul wrote, "and that is not your own doing. It is the gift of God, not of works, lest anyone should boast" (Ephesians 2:8,9).

St. Paul gave us the real power source in becoming a Christian. "No one can say, 'Jesus is Lord' except by the Holy Spirit" (1 Cor. 12:3). What this means is that the human will does not bring about the change; rather our human will gives permission to the Holy Spirit to make the changes inside us. The action is all from God but He cannot act without first having received permission from a willing candidate. No one ever became a Christian against his will or simply by his will. The free and unconditional consent of the will is essential to the new birth.

Thirdly, John says that nobody can do this for us. A "husband's will" cannot bring a wife into the kingdom of God, nor can a wife bring in the husband. The only believing and confessing that people can do is their own. And frankly, I am glad that this is so. It must please God immensely when a person decides to become a Christian. God honors the free will He gave each of us. When a person says yes to Jesus Christ he does so after making a free choice. This gives the yes its true meaning. It was selected as one of two options.

Last of all, there is the final step: receiving. What would you say if someone mentioned to you in February that the present you sent her for Christmas was still unwrapped? You would ask why. Presents are not to be admired but opened and appreciated and used.

Jesus comes to the front door of our hearts and minds NOT like the UPS deliveryman who is bringing a package. Christmas does not celebrate the world's getting a package; it celebrates the world's receiving a visit from the Maker of heaven and earth in human form! Jesus makes himself available but it is we who decide about inviting him in. Jesus used the familiar analogy: "Behold, I stand at the door and knock. If anyone hears my voice and opens the door I will come in and eat with him and he with me" (Rev. 3:20).

Did you catch the inclusiveness of that invitation? Those who are born into God's family are the "whosoevers" and "anyones" of the world. The only ones excluded are those who exclude themselves. We qualify for this new birth when we receive and believe in Jesus Christ, and choose to love and obey him. Here is what He promised: "If anyone loves me, he will obey my teaching. My Father will love him, and we will come to him and make our home with him" (John 14:23).

Phillips Brooks, in his famous Christmas carol, *O Little Town of Bethlehem*, put it memorably in these words:

"How silently, how silently, the wondrous gift is given!
So God imparts to human hearts the blessings of his heaven.
No ear may hear his coming but in this world of sin,
Where meek souls will receive him still the dear Christ enters in.
O Holy Child of Bethlehem, descend to us we pray.
Cast out our sin and enter in, be born in us today."

You may have celebrated many Christmases in your life but have never really opened God's original Christmas gift. Make this Christmas different. Let it mark not just the anniversary of Christ's physical birth but of **your spiritual birth.** If you are not sure you have ever received him and believed in him, do it now. Go over in ink, so to speak, what you may have written in pencil sometime ago when you did not really understand. Use the following prayer or one like it of your own making.

"Lord Jesus Christ, I now know the wonderful message of Christmas. I believe it and I want to make sure you are on the inside of the door of my heart, mind and soul. I agree with you that I have put self first and pursued happiness on my own terms. I believe you came into the world to pay for my sins on the cross and I thank you for this great gift of love. I accept your invitation to come into my life as Savior and I promise to follow you as Lord in the fellowship of your special family, the Church. Fill me with your Spirit and empower me to live for you starting right now and for the rest of my life. Amen."

If you have prayed such a prayer as this and meant what you said, you can be sure that Christ will honor it. He will come into your life as he has promised. Trust that promise, not your feelings, and claim for yourself the privileges of being in a special relationship with God. Then cultivate that relationship with him as you become connected with a congregation of believers where you will grow and mature in your faith. You will find that being a Christian is a matter of changing your whole perspective on how to pursue happiness. It will not be easy, but there is no greater reward than knowing for sure that you are right with God, and that you are pursuing a happiness which is genuine and will literally last forever.

I wish you the joy of the real Christmas
in celebration of the original Christmas gift...
God's gift of His Son Jesus Christ!

Footnotes

1   Page XII Lewis, C.S. *Miracles*, (New York: Macmillan Publishing Co. 1947), p. 108

2   Page 22 Packer, J.I., *Knowing God*, (Downers Grove, Ill.: InterVarsity Press 1973), p. 50

3   Page 24 Lewis, C. S., *Mere Christianity*, (New York: Macmillan Publishing Co., 1943) p. 140

4   Page 27 Lowry, Mark, *Mary Did You Know?*, *(Nashville, TN., J. Countryman 1998) p. 1*

5   Page 28 F.W. Pitt in *Portraits of Christ*, Henry Gariepy, ed., (Old Tappan, N.J., Fleming Revell Co., 1974) p. 25

6   Page 29 McGrath, Alister, *Understanding the Trinity*, (Grand Rapids, MI., Zondervan Publishing House, 1998), page 25

7   Page 35 Tozer, A.W., *Knowledge of the Holy, (New York, HarperCollins Publishers, 1961), p. 39*

8   Page 36 Packer, J.I., op.cit, p.50

9   Page 43 Zacharias, Ravi, *Jesus Among Other Gods*, (Nashville, TN: Word Publishing, 2000), page 38

10   Page 44 Lewis, C. S., *Miracles* (New York: Macmillan Publishing, 1947), *p. 59*

11   Page 45 Richardson, Alan, *A Dictionary of Christian Theology* (ed. by Alan Richardson, SCM Press, London, 1969) p. 357f.

12   Page 50 Erickson, Millard, *New Evangelical Theology*,,(London: Marshall, Morgan and Scott, 1968), p. 108

13   Page 50 Erickson, Millard, *The Word Became Flesh*, (Grand 0Rapids, Mich. Baker Books, 1991), p. 548

14   Page 52 Ibid. p. 550

15   Page 96 Allen, Alexander V. G., *The Life and Letters of Phillips Brooks (New York, N.Y. E. P. Dutton & Co., 1900), volume.II,* p. 871

16   Page 139 Taylor, Daniel, *"Deconstructing the Gospel of Tolerance"* in Christianity Today, Jan, 11th, 1999 Page 43

17   Page 153 Lewis, C. S. *Mere Christianity,* (New York, Macmillan, 1943), p. 167

18   Page 155 Luther, Martin, *"freedom of the Christian Man,"* quoted in *"History of Christianity,"* by Kenneth S. Latourette, (New York, Harper and Row Publishers, 1974) p. 715

19   Page 164 Phillips, J.B., *New Testament Christianity,* (London: Hodder and Stou0ghton, 1958), pp. 27-33

to order additional copies of

The Original
Christmas Gift

please call:

(800) 917-BOOK (2665)